The Book of Genesis Commentary (Chapters 1-11)

James Battell

Published by James Battell, 2024.

THE BOOK OF GENESIS COMMENTARY (CHAPTERS 1-11)

First edition. January 31, 2024.

ISBN: 979-8224124541

Written by James Battell.

Also by James Battell

The Shocking History of the Jesuits (The Society of Jesus)
King James I of England: The King The Vatican Could Not Kill
The Hidden Truth About Freemasonry, The Catholic Church, And
The Illuminati
Bible Prophecy Made Simple For Serious Students of Scripture
Did The Catholic Church Order Abraham Lincoln's Assassination?
Is Calvinism and the Doctrines of Grace Biblical?
The Book of Genesis Commentary (Chapters 1-11)
The Book of Genesis Commentary (Chapters 1-11)
Watchman Nee, Witness Lee, and Living Stream Ministry: A Critical
Analysis of Their Identity as Cult or Church
What Is Speaking In Tongues And Is It Still For Today?
Ephesians Bible Commentary
The Book of Romans Commentary
Philemon Bible Study (Slavery In Scripture)

CHAPTER 1

———

VERSE 1: "In the beginning God created the heaven and the earth."

First up, Genesis chapter 1 is very similar to the Gospel of John. John says: **"In the beginning was the Word, and the Word was with God, and the Word was God."** And on both occasions that word "beginning" is a reference to the beginning of time. This word "God" in Hebrew is Elohim, and it can be plural to mean gods and it can be singular to mean simply God. If we understand that word "God" to be a reference to the Trinity, which I believe that it is, then you will find the Trinity or Godhead right from the very beginning of the word of God.

Just before I go on to verse 2, I want to show you a couple of other things which may be of interest to you. Go to Job, Job 26. Keep in mind, like I say, that "God" is a reference to the Trinity or Godhead, so let's say in verse 1 of Genesis 1 that would be a reference to the Father – In the beginning the Father created the heaven and the earth, which is what the Nicene Creed says, but they omit the Son and the Holy Spirit. Look at Job 26:13: **"By his spirit he hath garnished the heavens; his hand hath formed the crooked serpent."** That, of course, is a reference to the Holy Spirit. So you've seen the Father and the Holy Spirit involved in the creation. Just look at verse 7: **"He stretcheth out the north over the empty place, and hangeth the earth upon nothing."** Now, that was written about 1500 BC. In fact, Job is the oldest book of the Bible, and here we find that this man Job, who some think was involved with the creation of the pyramids, has got a bit of prophecy here, which a lot of people didn't know until probably in the last 5-or 600 years that the earth was actually round. And people need to realise that this book is many, many years ahead of your average scientist or your average agnostic. It is a supernatural book, and it's divine in origin rather than human.

Just look at 25:4 before we move on, 25:4: **"How then can man be justified with God? or how can he be clean that is born of a woman?"** What a great question. The only way man is going to be justified, which means exonerated with God, would be for God to personally forgive His debt to Himself, and we'll look at that as we move on.

Okay. So the Holy Spirit, we see from Job 26, was involved with the creation; the Father was involved with the creation from Genesis chapter 1. Look at Colossians, Colossians chapter 1. The apostle Paul, the greatest Christian that ever lived – Jesus said that John the Baptist was the greatest up till His day, but those that came after John were even greater because the Kingdom was already here and they were entering in, whereas John was simply pointing people to the Kingdom. Okay. Colossians 1. Look at 14: **"In whom we have redemption through his blood, even the forgiveness of sins: Who is the image of the invisible God, the firstborn of every creature"** (vv. 14-15) I'll come back to that in a minute. **"For by him were all things created, that are in heaven, and that are in earth, visible and invisible, whether they be thrones, or dominions, or principalities, or powers: all things were created by him, and for him: And he is before all things, and by him all things consist"** (vv. 16-17.) So we've seen the Father involved with the creation of the entire solar system; we saw the Holy Spirit from Job 26 involved; and we've seen the Son involved from Colossians chapter 1.

As we are in Colossians, I want to quickly look at this expression **"the firstborn of every creature."** Nine times out of ten, if you get into a conversation with a Jehovah's Witness, he or she will take you to Colossians chapter 1, and I've seen a lot of Christians get tied up pretty quickly when we get to this bit of Holy Scripture. And they say, **"There you are. Jehovah God created Jesus. He was the firstborn of every creature."** Well, just a couple of points to show you here. First of all, this expression "firstborn" – actually as you look at 18: **"And he is the head of the body, the church: who is the beginning, the firstborn from the dead."** Now, if He was the firstborn from the dead chronologically, then what about Lazarus? What about the boy from Nain and the little girl from Mark 5, the *talitha cumi* child, the 12-year-old girl? If that's a chronological rendering, which you'd have to accept it to be if you want to go down the Jehovah's Witness route, then what do you do with that? But go back to 15: **"Who is the image of the invisible God, the firstborn of every creature:"** So therefore they say, **"Well, there you are. He's the firstborn in Jehovah's creation."** Well, we've already dealt with the chronological problem, but look at this "creature." Back to 18: **"who is the beginning, the firstborn from the dead; that in all things he might have the preeminence."** Okay. So this expression **"firstborn of every creature,"** if it's understood with verse 18, simply means He is the preeminence in order of creation.

But let's not stop there. Go to Psalm 89 – Scripture with Scripture – Psalm 89 verse 20: **"I have found David my servant; with my holy oil have I anointed him."** 27: **"Also I will make him my firstborn, higher than the kings of the earth."** Now, just keep this in mind that Jesse had eight sons, and David was the youngest of the eight sons, and yet this expression **"I'll make him my firstborn"** simply means he's going to be elevated in the mind of the Lord God. So when it says that Christ has the preeminence simply means that He is above everything in creation. And why would that be? Well, look at verse 16: **"all things were created by him"** (Col. 1:16.) If He made all things, He can't be a creation of His own creation, if that makes any sense.

So the quickest way to deal with the JWs, like I say, is to go to Psalm 89, and you can prove that David was the youngest of Jesse's sons, and yet when he's spoken of as the firstborn, it's in preeminence. And, of course, David is a type of Jesus Christ. Christ is the Son of David, and that's all that it means – that He has the preeminence. In fact, I'll show you one other Scripture quickly before I go on. Go to Philippians chapter 2, Philippians chapter 2:5: **"Let this mind be in you, which was also in Christ Jesus: Who, being in the form of God, thought it not robbery to be equal with God"** (vv. 5-6.) Now, how many people do you know that are equal with God? How many people can you point to in antiquity that claimed to be equal with God? You're not convinced? Go to John 10. It's not just the apostle Paul or Peter that believed that Christ was equal with the Lord. Go to John 10:33: **"The Jews answered him, saying, For a good work we stone thee not; but for blasphemy; and because that thou, being a man, makest thyself God."** Okay. Now, what Jesus was saying and doing was very quickly noted and seized upon by the Jews as being deity. To claim to be the Good Shepherd, to claim to be the Lord of the Sabbath, to claim to have power to forgive sins was, in their mind, a proclamation that He was Jehovah God, which He absolutely was.

And I'll show you one other Scripture quickly from John chapter 5:18: **"Therefore the Jews sought the more to kill him, because he not only had broken the Sabbath"** – which He hadn't done – **"but said also that God was his Father, making himself equal with God."** So there was no doubt in the mind of the Jews that He was deity, and, of course, that is why they put Him to death.

Back to Genesis chapter 1:

VERSE 2: "And the earth was without form, and void; and darkness was upon the face of the deep. And the Spirit of God moved upon the face of the waters."

Again, the Holy Spirit is mentioned in verse 2. Cross reference it to Job 20:26 and we've shown you the Son of God is also involved with the creation.

VERSE 3: "And God said, Let there be light: and there was light."

That expression to "lights" will be found ultimately in Jesus Christ. Christ said the Feast of Hanukkah, the Festival of Lights, which is the equivalent of Christmas – in most of Christendom, anyway – that He was the light of the world.

Okay. Just before we get back into a verse-by-verse exposition on Genesis, I want to give you a couple of scientific points which need to be highlighted. And the first up is how does the universe consist? And most scientists believe that the universe comes down to five components: Time, force, action, space, and matter. And it's amazing when you line that up with the word of God that they fit perfectly. Back to verse 1: **"In the beginning"** – time – **"God"** – force – **"created"** – action – **"the heaven"** – space – **"and the earth"** – matter. So there you have the unequivocal evidence that the Scripture fits in with the first five components of the universe. And it was Herbert Spencer in 1903 that first came to this conclusion. And, as I say, science and the Bible, the word of God, fit nicely.

One other thing I want to show you. Not everybody who is a scholar, not everybody who is an authority believes in evolution. I'm going to give you some quotes now. Sir Ambrose Fleming said the following: "Evolution is baseless and quite incredible"; Sir William Dawson: "Evolution is utterly destitute of proof"; Sir Fred Hoyle: "As a young student I was brainwashed into accounting everything without God"; Sir Francis Bacon: "Let no man think or maintain that a man can search too far or be too well studied in the book of God's Word or in the book of God's works"; Sir Bernard Lovell: "More scientists believe in creation than disbelieve." And it's an absolute fact that if you are a

Christian scientist and you believe in the creation account, then you will be frozen out of academia in the UK. The colleges and universities are funded by the taxpayer, and if you are a scientist, it's almost impossible to believe in creation and retain your job. And a lot of scientists have been not only humiliated, not only mocked, but some have even gone on to lose their jobs due to their intolerant colleagues.

And one other area I want to look at, and we'll get back to the Scripture. We have only four options to how the universe began and how it is still in place for today. Look at the first option: The universe came from nothing naturally, and that would violate the first law of thermodynamics because you cannot create energy or matter. Look at the second option: The universe came from nothing supernaturally, and that would fit with the Scriptures. Third option: The universe has always existed, and the problem with that is the second law of thermodynamics. Everything is breaking down, and it has been suggested by some that had the earth been here for 4 billion years, that everything would have burned out 35 million years ago. It's also worth pointing out that had man been on earth as long as some scientists believe, even with wars and sicknesses and everything else taken into consideration, we would have about 150,000 people per square inch, and there's no way that we could survive with that sort of ratio. And so that knocks out the third option. And the fourth option is the universe isn't real; it's just an illusion. And there are some people that take that position, but such people are normally confined to mental institutions. So there are your four options, and let me know what you think on that.

Okay. We looked at the Trinity working together as far as the creation of the world was concerned. I want to show you one other area where the three of them work together, and this will be in reference to the resurrection of the Lord Jesus Christ. Look at John 2:19: **"Jesus answered and said unto them, Destroy this temple, and in three**

days I will raise it up." "But he spake of the temple of his body" (v. 21.) So Jesus is quite clear that He was going to raise His body from the dead, which He did do, and He also said He had the power to lay His life down and take it up again. Go to Romans chapter 8 verse 11: **"But if the Spirit of him that raised up Jesus from the dead dwell in you, he that raised up Christ from the dead shall also quicken your mortal bodies by his Spirit that dwelleth in you."** So you saw the Son raise Him from the dead; you saw the Holy Spirit raise Him from the dead. Look at Galatians chapter 1 verse 1: **"Paul, an apostle, (not of men, neither by man, but by Jesus Christ, and God the Father, who raised him from the dead;)."** So there is a clear reference to the Father, the Son, and the Holy Spirit working independently while at the same time working together to resurrect the Lord Jesus Christ – three in one, one in three, and the one in the middle died for me.

Okay. I'm not quite finished yet. I want to show you three other areas that prove unequivocally that the Trinity are not only omnipotent, which as you know, means all powerful; omniscient, which means they can read people's minds and thoughts; and omnipresent, which means they are everywhere all at once — and, again, these are God-like features. There aren't any angels that come anywhere near these Scriptures I'm going to give you now. Okay. Let's start with God the Father. Go to 1 Peter. This will show you that the Godhead are omnipotent, all powerful, 1 Peter chapter 1 verse 5, God the Father in context: **"Who are kept by the power of God through faith unto salvation ready to be revealed in the last time."** Okay. That's quite clear. Go to 2 Corinthians chapter 12 verse 9, Jesus Christ in context: **"And he said unto me, My grace is sufficient for thee: for my strength is made perfect in weakness."** Go to Romans 15 in reference to the Holy Spirit, verse 19: "Through mighty signs and wonders, by the power of the Spirit of God." Okay. So you've seen that they are omnipotent.

Let's look at the omniscience. Again, that is a reference to being able to read people's minds and their hearts. Let's start with God the Father. Go to Jeremiah, Jeremiah 17:10: **"I the LORD"** – uppercase – **"search the heart, I try the reins, even to give every man according to his ways, and according to the fruit of his doings."** Okay. It's quite clear. Go to Revelation, Revelation chapter 2, a reference to Jesus – almost identical language. Revelation 2:23: **"And I will kill her children with death; and all the churches shall know that I am he which searcheth the reins and hearts: and I will give unto every one of you according to your works."** So that's crystal clear. As I say, it's almost word-for-word with Jeremiah. The Holy Spirit, go to 1 Corinthians chapter 2 verse 11: **"For what man knoweth the things of a man, save the spirit of man which is in him? even so the things of God knoweth no man, but the Spirit of God."**

And one more area, omnipresence, again, meaning to be everywhere at the same time. Only God has that feature. Even the devil doesn't come anywhere near this. Go to Jeremiah. This will be in reference to God the Father, Jeremiah 23:24: **"Can any hide himself in secret places that I shall not see him? saith the LORD"** – uppercase. **"Do not I fill heaven and earth? saith the LORD."** Amen. Go to Matthew, a reference to God the Son, Matthew 18 verse 20: **"For where two or three are gathered together in my name, there am I in the midst of them."** And the Holy Spirit, go to Psalm 139 verse 7: **"Whither shall I go from thy spirit? or whither shall I flee from thy presence? If I ascend up into heaven, thou art there: if I make my bed in hell, behold, thou art there."**

Okay. So you've seen unequivocally, I hope, that the Father, the Son, and the Holy Spirit are all omnipotent, omniscient, and omnipresent, and that, as I said, is clear evidence that the one God is not only the same but that each member of the Godhead is equal one to another.

And it is paramount that we understand that and believe it, not to mention teach it as correct Bible doctrine.

So back to Genesis chapter 1, we saw that God created the heaven and the earth, and that would be the entire solar system, and "God" in Genesis 1 would be a compound word for the Godhead, the triune God.

VERSES 2-3: "And the earth was without form, and void; and darkness was upon the face of the deep. And the Spirit of God moved upon the face of the waters – that's the Holy Ghost, of course. **"And God said, Let there be light: and there was light."**

Now, that could be a spiritual application to Jesus Christ, like I've already said. Jesus said He was the light of the world, and we can get into some of the types and shadows in Scripture as we go through this video. But I would say the first three verses, we've seen the Father, the Holy Ghost, and the Son in the creation. And, of course, as the Bible opens up, we find even more evidence to affirm that.

VERSE 4: "And God saw the light, that it was good" – Look at Matthew 3. Jesus is being baptized and God says, **"This is my beloved Son, in whom I am well pleased"** – very similar sort of language there. But here, of course, He's talking about the literal universe, the creation which still stands to this day - **"and God divided the light from the darkness."**

Now, this bit of Scripture, for me, makes it crystal clear that the light and the darkness would represent not only the sun and the moon but good and evil. Light would be a picture of redemption through the Lord Jesus Christ, and darkness would be a picture of death and judgment and ultimately Hell. And we have on day one, which we'll get to in verse 5, that the darkness and the light have already been created, and therefore Hell was made right at the beginning of creation. People say, "Well, what sort of God is this that creates a torture chamber for His people?" Go to Matthew 25. Now, just a bit of Scripture reading can make a lot of difference in people's soteriology and how they understand the Lord. Look at verse 41, Matthew 25:41: **"Then shall he say also unto them on the left hand, Depart from me, ye cursed, into everlasting fire, prepared for the devil and his angels."**

So Hell wasn't made for man; it was made for the devil. And some people argue that Satan had already fallen by Genesis chapter 1, and that would be a feed into the gap theory, hence why God needed to create Hell. A lot of people say, "Well, the Lord knew the devil was going to fall along with his minions, and therefore Hell was created to accommodate them." And, of course, Peter and Jude talk about them being chained, and they are still there to this day.

VERSE 5: "And God called the light Day, and the darkness he called Night. And the evening and the morning were the first day."

There are two areas of thought on this expression **"day."** There's the old earth people that say this period of day is thousands of years if not millions of years, and then there are the young earth people who take it to be a literal 24-hour day, and that is my position. I'm a young-earther, and I think the Bible can be proven to show that, and we'll get to that as we go on.

Okay. So day one He's made the light from the darkness, which would be the sun and the moon, and you've got a picture of the sun in verse 3, but the sun as it is as we see it today hasn't yet been created. So there's some kind of light – which I would say was probably Christ – bringing the universe into being, not only through His spoken word, but there's some other power there which we can't quite fathom in our own finite minds. And the Lord is going to ultimately create the sun, which we, as I say, still have to this day, although it's not as powerful as it used to be.

VERSES 6-8: "And God said, Let there be a firmament in the midst of the waters, and let it divide the waters from the waters. And God made the firmament, and divided the waters which were under the firmament from the waters which were above the firmament: and it was so. And God called the firmament Heaven. And the evening and the morning were the second day."

Now, we know there are three areas to heaven. If you are flying in an airplane, that is considered probably the first level of heaven. If you go into space like the Rapture, that would be a second layer of heaven, and if you go to be with the Lord Himself, that would be the third Heaven, which Paul speaks about in 2 Corinthians 12.

VERSES 9-11: "And God said, Let the waters under the heaven be gathered together unto one place, and let the dry land appear: and it was so. And God called the dry land Earth; and the gathering together of the waters called he Seas: and God saw that it was good. And God said, Let the earth bring forth grass, the herb yielding seed, and the fruit tree yielding fruit after his kind, whose seed is in itself, upon the earth: and it was so."

I just want to stop there. We saw the Garden of Eden from Revelation 21, 22, and the nations take of the tree for their healing. Now, of course, we haven't got to the creation of man and woman, but I want to make a quick point that before the fall, before man sinned, the whole of creation was vegetarian, as will be the same in the eternal state.

VERSE 12: "And the earth brought forth grass, and herb yielding seed after his kind, and the tree yielding fruit, whose seed was in itself, after his kind: and God saw that it was good."

One thing you will see verse after verse in Genesis is the Lord brings forth beast and tree and anything that He makes after its kind. And two terms which are put out in evolutionary circles is macroevolution and there's microevolution. And microevolution teaches the biblical account that dogs produce dogs, cats produce cats, so on and so forth, whereas macroevolution would say that a dog could produce a cat which could produce a rat which could produce a human being, and that is taught in every university all over the world. But the Bible doesn't understand that to be so. The Bible teaches microevolution, to bring forth fruit after its kind.

VERSE 13: "And the evening and the morning were the third day."

Now, again, there's no reason to doubt these are literal 24 hours of the day. These would be your literal lunar days.

VERSE 14: "And God said, Let there be lights in the firmament of the heaven to divide the day from the night; and let them be for signs, and for seasons, and for days, and years:"

That's going to be your stars, of course.

VERSES 15-16: "And let them be for lights in the firmament of the heaven to give light upon the earth: and it was so. And God made two great lights; the greater light to rule the day, and the lesser light to rule the night: he made the stars also."

That's quite obvious, the sun and the moon.

VERSES 17-20: "And God set them in the firmament of the heaven to give light upon the earth, And to rule over the day and over the night, and to divide the light from the darkness: and God saw that it was good. And the evening and the morning were the fourth day. And God said, Let the waters bring forth abundantly the moving creature that hath life, and fowl that may fly above the earth in the open firmament of heaven."

That fowl, of course, is a reference to birds, old English for birds.

VERSE 21: "And God created great whales, and every living creature that moveth, which the waters brought forth abundantly, after their kind, and every winged fowl after his kind: and God saw that it was good."

Now, some people – I'm thinking of theistic evolutionists, people who believe in a higher being - use this to prove macroevolution because it says that the living creatures are brought forth from the waters. But, of course, that's not what it means. It simply means that they mate in the water, and therefore they bring forth their own kind. So, once again, microevolution would be the correct term here, not macroevolution.

VERSE 22: "And God blessed them, saying, Be fruitful, and multiply, and fill the waters in the seas, and let fowl multiply in the earth."

I want to come back to that expression in a minute – fill in the earth – because in verse 28 we get into a bit of interesting Scripture. But here they're simply told to fill the waters and multiply in the earth.

VERSES 23-25: "And the evening and the morning were the fifth day. And God said, Let the earth bring forth the living creature after his kind" – again, microevolution – **"cattle, and creeping thing, and beast of the earth after his kind: and it was so. And God made the beast of the earth after his kind, and cattle after their kind, and every thing that creepeth upon the earth after his kind: and God saw that it was good."**

Okay. Now, the first several chapters we've seen day one right up to day five. And as you would imagine, the grass went down first, the literal seeds and trees. Then, of course, the animals came along bit by bit, the whales and all of the sea creation, and, of course, by 26, man arrives on the scene.

VERSE 26: "And God said, Let us make man in our image, after our likeness: and let them have dominion over the fish of the sea, and over the fowl of the air, and over the cattle, and over all the earth, and over every creeping thing that creepeth upon the earth."

Now, this should be quite obvious that Adam was the first man, and he had total dominion over the entire creation on the earth, and he even names the animals a little later on. But a lot of the animal rights people take great offence to this bit of Scripture. But the Lord wanted Adam to enjoy His creation, and, of course, what went with that was great power and great privilege.

VERSE 27: "So God created man in his own image, in the image of God created he him; male and female created he them."

And that is probably the most important part of Scripture after the birth, death, burial, and resurrection of Jesus Christ. If you are a Bible-believing Christian, you'll have to defend creation as and where you can. If we lose creation, then we've lost our witness; we've lost our testimony, because creation is absolutely paramount to biblical Christianity.

VERSE 28: "And God blessed them, and God said unto them, Be fruitful, and multiply, and replenish the earth" –

I just want to hold it there for a minute. Now, this expression **"replenish the earth,"** if you get any dictionary, the word "replenish" simply means to put in what was once there. And I was doing a quick study yesterday before I did this batch of videos just to see what other Bibles have the word **"replenish,"** and the Bishops' Bible is the only other Bible that I was able to find that had the word **"replenish."** And, of course, if you hold to the gap theory, which I don't, but if you do hold to the gap theory, this is probably your strongest bit of Scripture to prove, you'd have us believe, that man was once upon a time on the earth. And, of course, the gap theory doesn't teach man per se was on the earth but that the angels, the sons of God were on the earth. And there are some interesting arguments for the gap theory, which I won't get into now. But the Bishops' Bible, as I say, has the same word **"replenish."** All the other Bibles after the AV, the Authorised Version, put the word "fill" the earth. But here it has the expression "replenish the earth."

But go back to verse 21 and 22. Here you have the whales that are created, and they weren't told to replenish the earth. They were told to fill the earth. Now, it's possible that if you go for the gap theory that there weren't any waters and therefore hence why they wouldn't be told to refill what was once there. But verses 24 and 25, you have the cattle that are made, and they aren't told to replenish or even to multiply. So these groups of cattle, these groups of beasts, if they're just ordinary beasts, then you would expect them to be told to replenish or refill or to bring forth after their own kind. But they have a limited remit here, a limited mandate. They're not told to re-populate. So keep that in mind that this expression **"replenish"** is cited by the gap theorists, and, of course, those that don't hold to the gap theory would say it is a mistake, it shouldn't be there. And I don't believe in that either. I think it's there for a reason. But let's just say that the jury is out as of making this video as to what that should actually mean.

So back to 28: **"And God blessed them, and God said unto them, Be fruitful, and multiply, and replenish the earth and subdue it: and have dominion over the fish of the sea, and over the fowl of the air, and over every living thing that moveth upon the earth."**

What a great commission. The Lord's blessed them; He's made them, and He's given them a very clear mandate, and they are going to rule the world. Of course, that will be a greater fulfilment in the Millennium for the saved saint.

VERSE 29: "And God said, Behold, I have given you every herb bearing seed, which is upon the face of all the earth, and every tree, in the which is the fruit of a tree yielding seed; to you it shall be for meat."

Again, these are vegetarians, and the Lord has given them everything that they would need. Go to 1 Corinthians chapter 1. There are people that don't feel that they are equipped to do anything for the Lord. Look at verse 5: **"That in every thing ye are enriched by him, in all utterance, and in all knowledge."** So if you are already born again, you are completely equipped in Him to do whatever He wants you to do. Never mind a special commission; never mind having hands laid on you; never mind this or that. You're already totally enriched by Him, similar to what we see from the Garden of Eden.

VERSE 31: "And God saw every thing that he had made, and, behold, it was very good. And the evening and the morning were the sixth day."

This is the only part of Scripture where the Lord says **"it was very good,"** and for those that don't hold to the gap theory, we look at this and we find a perfect creation. We don't find any sin; we don't find anything that was uncalled for, and it's very difficult to think that had all this been made and the devil had already fallen and the angels had fallen too that the Lord would be saying it was very good. What the gap theorists will say is, **"Well, of course, this is the second creation,"** and that's where the gap theory comes into play. In the beginning God created the heaven and the earth, and they believe that's the first creation where Lucifer fell, and Isaiah 14 speaks about Lucifer and his seven "I am's" to ascend up into the heavens and to be the Lord Himself. And, of course, verse 2, **"And the earth was without form, and void,"** and they put the case forward that the break between these two verses is proof for the gap theory. Now, I'm not convinced of that, and maybe on another video we will go a little deeper into these two verses, these two breaks between 1:1 and 1:2. But for those that don't know, that is the position that the gap theorists hold to.

CHAPTER 2

VERSE 1: "Thus the heavens and the earth were finished, and all the host of them."

This expression **"host"** probably would be a reference to the angels. If you've read Genesis carefully, you will note that the angels aren't directly mentioned in the creation of the Lord, but the expression **"host"** normally refers to the armies of the Lord, the host of the Lord, the Lord of hosts. So I would take it to be a reference to the angelic world. And also it says the heavens were finished, and, of course, in Genesis 1:1, it was called **"the heaven"** singular, and that expression **"heaven,"** like I've already said, refers to not only heaven as we see it today from earth but the entire solar system. And there are three levels to heaven: The third Heaven is where the Lord dwells; the second heaven would be in space itself where the spacecraft, the Apollos and all your NASA's ships, planes – whatever they are – that would be your second heaven, and, of course, the first heaven would be where you are today. If you're flying on a plane somewhere, that would be considered the first heaven.

VERSES 2-3: **"And on the seventh day"** – which, of course, would be Saturday – **"God ended his work which he had made; and he rested on the seventh day from all his work which he had made. And God blessed the seventh day, and sanctified it: because that in it he had rested from all his work which God created and made."**

Now, obviously the expression "seventh day" appears three times in just two verses. That is very important. And the Lord has set that day apart as a picture for rest, and, of course, later that would be given to the Jews, and the Sabbath was a sign between Jehovah God and the children of Israel. And I've done a video on the Sabbath before, so I won't go over that again. But nonetheless, here you find a picture of what the Sabbath is going to become, but it doesn't become an issue until probably around about the time of Moses.

VERSE 4: "These are the generations of the heavens and of the earth when they were created, in the day that the LORD God made the earth and the heavens,"

Now, the old-earth people take this expression **"in the day"** to be a reference to a period of time. They don't understand Genesis to be teaching that the whole world came into place on one day - which it could have done - so they say, "There you are. That expression 'in the day' would be a reference to a period of time." Now, I don't go for that. In Acts 17 the Scripture says that God has chosen a day when He would judge the world. That's simply an expression. It's like saying there was a day when England was great, and it's not a literal 24-hour day; it's a period of time. And when Christ judges the world, He's going to judge the world on a literal day, a literal 24-hour day – what He might do - but it could be a reference to a period of time. But here in the creation, we've already seen – I mean, just go back to it. Genesis 1:5, day 1; verse 8, day 2; verse 13, day 3; verse 19, day 4; 23, day 5; 31, day 6. I mean, the Bible breaks it down to day one right up to day six.

So you can't use verse 4 to somehow overthrow these literal 24-hour days, if we even knew the Jewish calendar days. It doesn't matter. They're still literal days. You can't go to verse 4 and force that to teach an old-earth theory, and I'll show you from verse 5 why you can't do that. But I just wanted to show you that point, because there are people who don't like the six-day account, and they don't like it because they want to fit in with the scientists, the brains, the great scholars, and they also want to hold to the belief in a higher being. And that is theistic evolution, and we don't go for that. We believe that the Lord is eternal, and at a period of time, He brought the earth into being; and He not only made the earth, but He's sustaining it even to this day.

VERSE 5: "And every plant of the field before it was in the earth, and every herb of the field before it grew: for the LORD God had not caused it to rain upon the earth, and there was not a man to till the ground."

Now, just bear with me. Actually, look at verse 6:

VERSE 6: "But there went up a mist from the earth, and watered the whole face of the ground."

Okay. So let's just say these days from verse 5 right over to verse 31, let's just say they're not literal 24-hour days but they are periods of decades or even centuries, some people would have you believe. You've got the grass that's been planted; you've got the trees in the ground, and you've got man on the ground. How long can trees and grass and mankind survive without water? Is it not three, four days without water? If you had a thousand years for each period of the account, if you had a thousand years for day one, a thousand years for day two right up to day six, that's – what? – 6,000 years – you're going to have a lot of dead wood literally; you're going to have Adam and Eve dying because they've got no water to drink. No. It can't be taken to be long periods of time. It would have to be taken to be literal 24-hour days.

VERSE 7: "And the LORD God" – This is the first time we find **"LORD God."** Of course, LORD would be Jehovah in the Latin, which came out of the Vulgate, which is found three or four times in the King James, and the Hebrew expression would be Yahweh. **"And the LORD God formed man of the dust of the ground, and breathed into his nostrils the breath of life; and man became a living soul."**

Now, that expression, again, **"LORD God"** would be a reference to the Trinity, I believe, and I've shown you from other Scriptures that it wasn't just the Lord as God the Father doing this, as the Nicene Creed would have you believe, but the triunity of God, the triune God. He makes man from the dust of the ground. Again, there's no evolution here. He just makes him; He speaks him into being.

VERSE 8: "And the LORD God planted a garden eastward in Eden; and there he put the man whom he had formed."

Most people think that Eden is probably in Iraq somewhere, and I would say that's probably the case, but I'm open to suggestions if it's not.

VERSE 9: "And out of the ground made the LORD God to grow every tree that is pleasant to the sight, and good for food; the tree of life also in the midst of the garden, and the tree of knowledge of good and evil."

Okay. So it's two trees which have been marked out. There's probably other trees, but these are the two main trees. And, again, there's no evolution here. The Lord is creating something from nothing as only He can do.

VERSE 10: "And a river went out of Eden to water the garden; and from thence it was parted, and became into four heads."

Look at Revelation, Revelation 21 verse 1: **"And I saw a new heaven and a new earth: for the first heaven and the first earth were passed away; and there was no more sea."** Look at 22 verse 1: **"And he shewed me a pure river of water of life, clear as crystal, proceeding out of the throne of God and of the Lamb."** So we know in the Millennium going into the eternal state there will be no more sea but there will be rivers, and it's interesting in Genesis chapter 2 that the river is going to come out of Eden, which, as I say, is quite possibly modern-day Iraq.

Eleven talks about gold; **12** talks about bdellium and the onyx stone; **13** talks about the whole land encompassing Ethiopia, which, of course, is Africa; **14** talks about the third river and that is towards Assyria, and the fourth river comes out of Euphrates, which, of course, is Iraq. And Iraq will quite possibly play a major role in the last days.

VERSE 15: "And the LORD God took the man, and put him into the garden of Eden to dress it and to keep it."

Now, of course, Eden was perfect, absolutely no problems as of this stage. Original sin hasn't occurred. And as we go through the next few verses, we see that Adam has got a lot more responsibility than was first thought.

VERSES 16-17: "And the LORD God commanded the man, saying, Of every tree of the garden thou mayest freely eat: But of the tree of the knowledge of good and evil, thou shalt not eat of it: for in the day that thou eatest thereof thou shalt surely die."

Now, when we look at this Scripture, people say, "Did Adam eat of the tree?" Yes, he did. Did he die? No, he didn't. And people like to cause a contradiction. They like to cause a controversy, when, of course, the Scripture says the wages of sin is death, and you will die in your sin if you're not saved.

Go to 1 Corinthians. I'll come back to Genesis in a minute. First Corinthians 11:28: **"But let a man examine himself"**; **"he that eateth and drinketh unworthily, eateth and drinketh damnation to himself"**; **"For this cause many are weak and sickly among you, and many sleep."** Of course, that is a reference to dying sleep. Lazarus with asleep from John 11, but he wasn't having a snooze; he was dead; he was four days dead by the time Christ got to him and resurrected him.

And here you have a reference to saved people that have died in their sin, but they haven't gone to Hell because they've already had their resurrection.

Look at Ephesians 2, Ephesians 2:6: **"And hath raised us up together"** – present tense – **"and made us sit together in heavenly places in Christ Jesus."** When you believed on the Lord, truly believed – not just a "one, two, three, pray with me" – but when you truly believed and received Christ, you were baptized into His death, Romans 6, and look at John 5:24. So that's one of the deaths that is in mind here.

VERSE 18: "And the LORD God said, It is not good that the man should be alone; I will make him an help meet for him."

Now this, of course, has been used over the years to make it crystal clear that man, as and where he can, should be married, should be with wife. And if you've got a church leadership team, if you will, it's normally healthy if you've got a couple of married elders or deacons running the church. Go to 1 Timothy, 1 Timothy 3:1: **"This is a true saying, If a man desire the office of a bishop, he desireth a good work."** Now, of course, we know the word **"bishop"** has been abused in the Anglican or Catholic churches. A bishop, as you well know, is a man who's a bachelor, especially if he is a Catholic, and he's responsible for many churches. But in the New Testament, a bishop is a married man, and it's unfortunate that the high churches have kind of hijacked this word bishop. But the New Testament does say he was a married man; he was blameless; he was sober, of good behaviour, given to hospitality, apt to teach.

Now look at 3: **"Not given to wine."** Now, how many bishops, how many deacons do you know that like a good drink? We've seen these people over the years sitting in the street knocking back the booze, and it just ruins your testimony, and it causes weak Christians to stumble. And we've dealt with this in previous videos. But if you are a Christian and you have a taste for alcohol and for whatever reason you haven't yet got control over it, don't drink in public. Everything you do is seen. And the same goes with smoking, as well. In fact, anything that would cause a weak Christian to sin due to your liberty is an absolute no-no.

Verse 4: **"One that ruleth well his own house, having his children in subjection with all gravity."** So you see the bishop here is a married man with children, and there are no married bishops with children in the Catholic church, at least not officially. We know back in the early 1990s, 5,000 vicars left the Church of England due to women priests being allowed in through the Synod. The Synod voted, and a load of women joined the church, and 5,000 exited the church, and they left with their wives and children. And the deal was that the children would go to private schools, which in the UK are about 8- to 12,000 pounds a year per child, and also they got private medicine. And in some countries it's different, but in the UK, we have the National Health Service, which is a pretty good system. It's not perfect, but it's better than most countries. And we have an organisation called Bupa, which is private medicine, and it's really for those that have money; and if you haven't got any money, then they're not interested in helping you. So all these vicars and wives came with them, and their children came with them, and the deal was when your wives die, you cannot remarry, which is interesting. But nonetheless, the early church would expect an elder to have a wife and children.

So we go back to Genesis, Genesis 2:18: **"And the LORD God said, It is not good that the man should be alone; I will make him an help meet for him."** Now, just keep this also in mind that the apostle Paul, as far as we know – and there's no evidence to suggest otherwise – but as far as we know, he wasn't married. Now, some people say he was a widower. Well, maybe he was, but that's just speculation.

The apostle John was a young man when the Lord died, and he took Mary and her children into his home. Of course, Christ was the oldest of the children, so His responsibility would have been delegated to John; and Mary, along with her young children, whatever age they were at the time, moved into the apostle John's house. There's no evidence that John was married.

So it's not mandatory to be married with children to be in a position of leadership in your local assembly, but the groundwork, the foundation is laid with the understanding that you probably will have a wife and children.

VERSE 19: "And out of the ground the LORD God formed every beast of the field, and every fowl of the air; and brought them unto Adam to see what he would call them: and whatsoever Adam called every living creature, that was the name thereof."

Now, when I look at this Scripture, I wonder to myself, not only did Adam name all of the animals – and as we go through Scripture, they are given names. Secular history comes along, picks up these names. It's interesting – isn't it? – how they follow the Bible. But I wonder if Adam spoke to the animals. I think we've all seen Doctor Doolittle, a 1960s film with - I think it was Rex Harrison talking to the animals, and it was quite a unique film at the time. But I wonder if Adam had the ability to talk to the animals.

VERSE 20: "And Adam gave names to all cattle, and to the fowl of the air, and to every beast of the field; but for Adam there was not found an help meet for him."

It's quite possible that these animals that the Lord initially created – this is, of course, before the fall of man and the flood and everything else – some of these animals may well have died in the flood. In fact, if you go back to Genesis 1:24: **"And God said, Let the earth bring** forth the living creature after his kind, cattle, and creeping thing, and beast of the earth after his kind: and it was so" – again, microevolution, not macro. Twenty-five: **"And God made the beast of the earth after his kind, and cattle after their kind, and every thing that creepeth upon the earth after his kind: and God saw that it was good."** It's quite possible that some of these cattle, some of these beasts that the Lord made didn't actually make it post flood, and that's why they're not told to repopulate the earth – just a little hypothesis of mine. It's not going to be a matter of dogma but just a thought that I've got.

Look at the second part of verse 20: **"but for Adam there was not found an help meet for him."** Of course, **"meet"** is old English for mate.

VERSES 21-22: "And the LORD God caused a deep sleep to fall upon Adam, and he slept: and he took one of his ribs, and closed up the flesh instead thereof; And the rib, which the LORD God had taken from man, made he a woman, and brought her unto the man."

Of course, "woman" comes from "man" – wo-man – man with a womb and it's interesting that she comes from his rib. Women's lib – excuse the pun – have always had problems with the role of women in the Scripture, and they suggest that she is insubordinate to man, which she's not, and that the Lord is a misogynist, which He's not, and they have never really been able to deal with the Bible's presentation that men and women have different roles. And we've spoken about this in other videos that in the body of Christ for today, we are all, according to Galatians 1, the same. There's neither male nor female, Greek nor Gentile. But practically, roles will fluctuate. Not all women are able to be child-bearers and not all men are able to be fathers.

And it's the same in the church. If you're in a local assembly or a house church, not everybody in that setting will be able to exegete the

Scriptures, to go through it verse by verse. Not everybody in the local church would be able to street preach or do apologetic work. And the same with women. Women are not given the position of leadership, and it's my belief that when the Judgment Seat of Christ comes around, all of those faithful women that knew they weren't to be Bible teachers will be clapping their hands with joy because James says that let us not all be many masters (Js. 3:1.) It will be a blessing to these women that they won't have to give an account of themselves for some of the things they taught over the years when it came to Scripture. But nonetheless, the Bible doesn't show any distinctions, and Scripture also says that God is no respecter of persons (Acts 10:34.)

VERSE 23: "And Adam said, This is now bone of my bones, and flesh of my flesh: she shall be called Woman, because she was taken out of Man."

Again, the New Testament says that we are bone of His bone, flesh of His flesh. So there are parallels between Adam – and he, of course, is a type of Christ – and his wife Eve, which is a type of the church. And she comes out from him to become the equivalent to him, but, of course, in female form.

VERSE 24: "Therefore shall a man leave his father and his mother, and shall cleave unto his wife: and they shall be one flesh."

Now, this is a good Scripture to use to show the Trinity. Here you have a man and a woman coming together and becoming one flesh, but they're still two individuals but they're one flesh. Now, it's a paradox, of course, but it reflects the Trinity. You have three members of the Godhead but one God. Jesus was baptized in Matthew chapter 3, and the Holy Spirit comes from Heaven and the Father speaks, and you get three individual members of the Godhead all doing something simultaneously. Now, some people that are Modalists will try and go around this and say, "Well, God is able to reveal Himself in three separate personalities without being three separate persons." The Oneness people will say that the Father is Jesus, the Holy Spirit is Jesus, and, of course, Jesus would be Jesus Himself. It gets very confusing if you're not a Trinitarian because, in essence, you have the Father talking to Himself if you're a Oneness, but if you're a Trinitarian, then we see Jesus in the Garden praying to His Father, and in John 12 He says, **"Father, glorify thy name,"** and God glorifies His name. We know that the Son of God is talking to His Father, and, of course, the Father speaks to the Son. So with Trinitarianism, these aren't problems at all, but if you're not a Trinitarian, then you have to do cartwheels to get these Scriptures to make any sense.

VERSE 25: "And they were both naked, the man and his wife, and were not ashamed."

One of the most unnatural things that you'll see today is these nudist camps, and there's quite a few in the UK. And these people who are interviewed on television, they try and justify their dancing around, or if you're a pagan, go around a tree naked as if it's somehow normal and somehow natural; and, of course, it's not normal and it's not natural. Now, some people are being given over to a reprobate mind, so they think it's quite normal and quite acceptable. But society on the whole will tell you that it's not normal or natural, and yet here, again, before the fall of man, Adam and Eve are both naked and they are not ashamed.

Okay. Just before I get on to the third chapter, I have a couple of things I want to just show you from Genesis chapter 2 verse 21: **"And the LORD God caused a deep sleep to fall upon Adam, and he slept: and he took one of his ribs, and closed up the flesh instead thereof."** Now, first up, this is the first record in Scripture of an operation taking place. Paul speaks about a spiritual operation in the New Testament, but here we find a physical operation. And it's also one of two occasions when the Lord puts two different people to sleep. The first, of course, is Adam here, and he awakes to find he has a wife, who isn't named until the third chapter, and I'll come to that in a minute. And the second reference, of course, is to Abraham, and he awoke and found he had an unconditional covenant, which, of course, was the land of Israel. This sleeping in the New Testament would be a reference to a saved person sleeping in the Lord, of course, dying in the Lord and awaiting the resurrection.

Go back to 17: **"But of the tree of the knowledge of good and evil, thou shalt not eat of it: for in the day that thou eatest thereof thou shalt surely die."** Adam ate of the fruit along with his wife, and they both died. But he didn't die physically straightaway. In fact, we know from the latter part of Genesis that he lived to about 900 plus years. So this isn't a physical death; this is a spiritual death. And although the Bible does say that the wages of sin is death, that can be a reference to a saved person or even an unsaved person. Here we are looking at a spiritual death, and, as I say, the Lord prolonged it for many, many years.

In Genesis chapter 3, verse 21, it says the LORD God made coats of skins and clothed them, and some commentators see this as a type of an imputed righteousness which is given to the saved man and woman when they believe on the Lord Jesus Christ. In fact, even in the Old Testament they got a temporary covering, of course, through Christ's future righteousness, but there are some Christians who believe that Adam and Eve died and didn't go to Heaven, they weren't saved. And my understanding of the Scripture would be that they probably were saved and this covering of skins would be a type of the imputed righteousness which we get from the New Testament.

Go back to verse 21: **"And the LORD God caused a deep sleep to fall upon Adam, and he slept..."** Now, this reference to sleeping in the

New Testament is used to explain death. Sleeping and death are used interchangeably, and I'll just show you a couple of references. In Acts 7:60 in reference to Stephen, it says, **"And he kneeled down, and cried with a loud voice, Lord, lay not this sin to their charge. And when he had said this, he fell asleep."** The same sort of language is found in John chapter 11 in reference to Lazarus. And in 1 Corinthians – I'll give you one more Scripture – it says, **"For this cause many are weak and sickly among you, and many sleep"** (1 Cor. 11:30.) This is a reference to carnal Christians, and, yes, they do exist. I know Lordship salvation people would tell you that they do not exist, but the Bible says that they do. And if you look at verse 29, **"For he that eateth and drinketh unworthily, eateth and drinketh damnation to himself, not discerning the Lord's body."** Look at 31: **"For if we would judge ourselves, we should not be judged. But when we are judged, we are chastened of the Lord, that we should not be condemned with the world"** (v. 32.) So this sleeping that we find in the book of Genesis, although it was only a short sleep for maybe a few hours or so, at least spiritually we could apply this to the resurrection of the saved sinner - you die, you go to sleep, and you await the resurrection.

Okay. One other point just to squeeze in. Look at verse 22, Genesis 2:22: **"And the rib, which the LORD God had taken from man, made he a woman, and brought her unto the man."** Not only does she come from man, but look at chapter 3, verse 20: **"And Adam called his wife's name Eve ..."** So not only did he name the animals, he also names his wife because she was the mother of all living. Now, just think this through for a minute. This bit of Scripture was written 1500 BC, a good 1500 years before Jesus Christ was born. The events in this book go back even further than that. We know from western civilisation that every woman, every girl that is born takes her father's name, which is her maiden name, and when she gets married, she takes her husband's name; and if they have children, the children take the father's name – almost identical to the book of Genesis. Even if she's not living with the man that she has children with, she still allows her children to take the father's name. So the Bible says that Adam named his wife, and in secular society, even in 2010, women all over the world are taking their father's name or their husband's name. So, once again, we find that the Bible sets the standard, and secular society unknowingly follows it through because the Lord is the Master of the universe. He sets the rules; He sets the perimeters, and everybody, whether they realise it or not, follow along.

One final point I want to make before I close this video. It's the unfounded and unfair claim that women are somehow discriminated against in the Scriptures. And I challenge anybody watching this video anywhere in the world to show me any religion from antiquity that gave women the rights that the word of God gives them. We know from the first five books of the Bible – just as a quick side point – that the Jews, the children of Israel, were not only given do's and don'ts from the Ten Commandments, which – surprise, surprise – every civilised nation still uses to this day, but they also gave the Jews, the children of Israel, God's chosen people, a bill of rights clearly laid out in the first five books of the Bible, and you won't find that in any other religion anywhere in the world. But I want to give you some Scriptures just before I sign out. Go to Matthew 28. And the most important event after the creation of the world is the birth, death, burial, and the resurrection of the Lord Jesus Christ. And in Matthew 28 the first person to get to see the risen Christ was not Mary, mother of the Lord Jesus Christ, so-called Queen of Heaven; it wasn't Peter, so-called Pope of Rome, but in Matthew 28 verse 1 it says, **"In the end of the sabbath, as it began to dawn toward the first day of the week, came Mary Magdalene ..."** She was the first person to see the risen Saviour, and in John's Gospel, John chapter 20, Jesus says to her in verse 17, **"Touch me not; for I am not yet ascended to my Father: but go to my brethren, and say unto them, I ascend unto my Father, and your Father; and**

to my God, and your God.” This is the Great Commission, and it's given to a woman.

Some people say, "Well, wasn't Jesus married to Mary Magdalene?" Well, if He was married to her, you would have thought that the New Testament writers would write this. Go to 1 Corinthians 9 verse 5: **"Have we not power to lead about a sister, a wife, as well as other apostles, and as the brethren of the Lord, and Cephas?"** Well, Peter was married and so were the brothers of the Lord. But had Christ Himself been married, wouldn't Paul have put that down and cited Jesus' marriage for grounds that he could marry too? No. If the Lord had been married, it would have gone in the Scripture. It's not in the Scripture because He wasn't married, and all these books that have come out in recent years are simply rehashing old heresies about the blood line that allegedly goes back to the Lord Jesus Christ and Mary Magdalene.

And I'll say one other quick point. Had Christ married Mary Magdalene and gone and lived in the south of France, as some writers suggest He did, then wouldn't the apostles have known that? And had they known that, why would they have all been martyred for their faith? All of the apostles but one died for their faith in the Lord Jesus Christ. And just to deal with those that would say, "Well, the Bible is written by man and we can't trust it; they are biased towards the events of the Lord Jesus Christ, and they were out to start a new religion," look at Matthew 28:17: **"And when they saw him, they worshipped him: but some doubted."** Now, why would you put that latter part in that some doubted if this is a book written to convince people of an event that wasn't so? If it was all a hoax, why would you put in there that some doubted? I believe it was put in there to reflect the honesty and integrity of the Gospel writers, and it just shows you that even saved people won't shy away from telling you the truth about the Lord Jesus Christ.

So my final point would be that Mary Magdalene was allowed to see the resurrected Christ, and she's a type of fallen woman, if you will. Eve fell, and all women have partaken of her sufferings through childbirth and all the other problems that women claim to have. And the Lord allowed Mary Magdalene, of all people, to see His resurrection. And if anybody thinks that the Bible puts women down, then I ask you to go back to the Gospels and ask yourselves, "Why would it be that the Lord allowed a woman, Mary Magdalene – not the apostles, not Peter, not John – but He allowed a woman to witness His resurrection?" And it was done, as I understand it, to reverse the stigma that Eve experienced back in the Garden of Eden.

CHAPTER 3

VERSE 1: "Now the serpent was more subtil than any beast of the field which the LORD God had made. And he said unto the woman, Yea, hath God said, Ye shall not eat of every tree of the garden?"

Now, first up, I want to make it crystal clear that the reference here to a serpent is not just to a snake, per se, but it's who is behind the snake. There are times in the Scriptures when the Lord will speak to a particular person, but He's talking to the spirit behind the person. Go to Matthew 16 verse 23: **"But he turned, and said unto Peter, Get thee behind me, Satan: thou art an offence unto me: for thou savourest not the things that be of God, but those that be of men."** Look at 18: **"And I say also unto thee, That thou art Peter, and upon this rock I will build my church; and the gates of hell shall not prevail against it."** So in 18 He's blessing Peter with His proclamation of who He was, and if you read the whole of chapter 16, He does ask all the apostles, "Who do you all say that I am?" And, of course, Peter speaks for all of them because he was probably the oldest. But nonetheless, he says upon the rock, which, of course, is Himself, and it was Peter's profession of faith that is in reference here, not Peter himself. But nonetheless, Peter is commended here in verse 18, and He says in 17, **"Blessed art thou, Simon Barjona: for flesh and blood hath not revealed it unto thee, but my Father which is in heaven."** So as I say, Peter was commended here, but by 23, He's saying, **"Get thee behind me, Satan."**

Now, some Christians believe that it is possible for saved people to be demon-possessed or devil-possessed, and I don't believe that myself, but there are some – not many, but there are some that hold to that position. So in 23 the Lord Jesus Christ isn't just talking to Peter, but He's talking to the spirit behind Peter, that being Satan himself. So I just wanted to show that to you.

Go back to Genesis chapter 3, and it says that the Lord God had made the serpent, and he was more subtle than any beast of the field. Go to Ezekiel 28. Like I said, this isn't just a serpent, per se; it's who is behind the serpent. Ezekiel 28:13: **"Thou hast been in Eden the garden of God; every precious stone was thy covering"; 14: "Thou art the anointed cherub that covereth; and I have set thee so: thou wast upon the holy mountain of God; thou hast walked up and down in the midst of the stones of fire"; 15: "Thou wast perfect in thy ways from the day that thou wast created, till iniquity was found in thee."** That, of course, is a reference to Lucifer, the light-bearer from Isaiah 14; and, of course, Lucifer is Satan, and Satan is the devil – same person, just different titles. And I wanted to make that crystal clear because there are people who don't get demonology very clear in their own minds, and they think that Jesus and Satan are somehow spirit brothers, and if you don't know who I'm referring to, it is, of course, the Latter Day Saints.

Jesus is eternal, as I've shown you in other videos – Micah 5:2 would be the quickest verse to take you to – and I've just shown you that the devil was created, and now he says unto Eve, **"Hath God said, You should not eat of every tree of the garden?"** Interesting that he goes to Eve and not Adam, and people will say that the women are the weaker vessel, which the Scripture says that they are, and therefore they are prone to some kind of deception. In fact, if you go to 1 Timothy – New Testament, of course – 1 Timothy chapter 2:12: **"But I suffer not a woman to teach, nor to usurp authority over the man, but to be in silence. For Adam was first formed, then Eve. And Adam was not deceived, but the woman being deceived was in the transgression. Notwithstanding she shall be saved in childbearing, if they**

continue in faith and charity and holiness with sobriety" (vv. 12-15.) So here the woman is told to have children, to keep the house, and if she does that, she won't be deceived through deception, not salvation. Some people think this is a reference to salvation and therefore they say you have to be married with children to be saved, which is nonsense. Anna from the Gospel of Luke wasn't with children and she wasn't married; she'd been a widow for many years, and yet she was saved. And there's other women in the Bible that weren't with children and they were nonetheless saved.

Also, I think it's quite fair to say this wasn't the first time that the serpent had spoken to Eve. Some familiarity had obviously built up over the years, and he was able to approach her on probably more than one occasion. Also, from Genesis 2 to Genesis 3, there's no doubt a gap. It's difficult to know how long it's been, but for those that don't hold to the gap theory, the position is put forward that between Genesis 2 and 3, the devil has fallen; he's fallen through pride. He wanted to be like the Lord, and some have even said that he was jealous that Adam was the first man and Adam was getting all this attention – just a theory that some people put out.

VERSES 2-3: "And the woman said unto the serpent, We may eat of the fruit of the trees of the garden: But of the fruit of the tree which is in the midst of the garden, God hath said, Ye shall not eat of it, neither shall ye touch it, lest ye die."

Again, that's a slight abbreviation from verse 17 in the second chapter. Also, I wanted to say this that we don't talk to demons or devils. The apostle Paul did so in Acts – I think it was Acts 17, but Paul was an apostle. Paul was dealing with a demon-possessed woman. He'd been to the third Heaven; he'd been personally commissioned by Jesus Christ, and he said that he had all knowledge, and he was totally equipped for that part of his ministry. And it was a very limited ministry as also needs pointing out. We know by the end of Paul's life that the healings had dried up, the visions had dried up, and he even says in – I think it's Galatians that he didn't know who these people were that were harming the Galatians with their false teachings, and yet in earlier parts of the epistles, he had all knowledge of everything.

So we don't get into this binding the devil and binding these demons and talking and so on and so forth. That comes under hyper-charismatics, and even moderate Pentecostals have this binding and talking to the devil, and that's probably one of the main reasons why so many Christians are screwed up because they are talking to spirits, and they have no need to do so. And in verses 2 and 3, Eve is talking to the serpent, and she says she can eat of the fruit of the trees in the garden but the one in the middle she cannot eat, and as the Lord had already told, in the day you do so, you will surely die. And the serpent says to her you will not die. So here you find the first contradiction to what the Lord has already said. Jesus said the devil was a liar and a murderer from the beginning, and this is why it's paramount that if you're a Bible-believing Christian that you read the Scriptures daily, and everybody who comes to you and anybody who tries to distract you or lead you away, you need to check them out in light of Scripture. Sola Scriptura simply means that the Scripture is the final authority, and we've said in other videos, without this Book, you are totally lost.

VERSE 4: "And the serpent said unto the woman, Ye shall not surely die:"

His first and fatal lie to mankind.

VERSE 5: "For God doth know that in the day ye eat thereof, then your eyes shall be opened, and ye shall be as gods, knowing good and evil."

Now, this part of Scripture is interesting and it's also confusing – it's confusing because this reference to "gods," lower case "g," simply means you could be Godlike. One of the promises throughout antiquity right up to the current day is that man can one day become gods, and the Mormon church, the Latter Day Saints, are very keen on promoting this in their temple and with their Masonic secret rituals. But also it could be a reference to God Himself, which we find in the latter part of chapter 3. But the King James has translated it "gods," lower case "g," and I will bow to their superior knowledge of the Hebrew and leave it as it stands.

But the second part, **"knowing good and evil,"** now, of course, this expression "good and evil" is what original sin is. I was talking to a man just yesterday on the street, and he wanted to get into a debate with me on Christianity and so on and so forth. And we got onto original sin, and I said to him, "Well, you will be judged by the Ten Commandments because you know the difference between good and evil, you can choose one over the other." When Adam was made, all he knew was perfection, but by verse 5, the reality of original sin is to know good from evil.

VERSE 6: "And when the woman saw that the tree was good for food, and that it was pleasant to the eyes, and a tree to be desired to make one wise, she took of the fruit thereof, and did eat, and gave also unto her husband with her; and he did eat."

This is the thing about lust – you covet, you lust, and then you take. Lot was a lustful man, and yet the Bible says he was a just man. He was a righteous man, but he was lustful, nonetheless. David lusted after Bathsheba, and the Lord killed their child, and his whole family went into meltdown. All of his days up till his death there was discord in his family over one night of lust with Bathsheba.

VERSE 7: "And the eyes of them both were opened, and they knew that they were naked; and they sewed fig leaves together, and made themselves aprons."

Very important this, I said at the end of chapter 2, that people who go to nudist camps and promote it as being normal are actually deceived. In the New Testament one of the signs of a demon-possessed person is that they run around naked. And here Adam and Eve are now of the mindset that their sin has found them out, and they want to cover themselves up, which is quite normal.

VERSE 8: "And they heard the voice of the LORD God walking in the garden in the cool of the day: and Adam and his wife hid themselves from the presence of the LORD God amongst the trees of the garden."

This is a very interesting part of Scripture because it shows the innocency and the childlike nature of Adam and Eve hiding themselves. It's a bit like a delinquent child who is in the wrong and the parent is looking for the child – very similar.

VERSE 9: "And the LORD God called unto Adam, and said unto him, Where art thou?"

This is really important. The Bible says that God in the person of Jesus Christ came to seek and to save that which was lost. In fact, if you go to John 12 – Calvinists like to make a big noise about John 6:44 that nobody can come to God unless the Father draw him. Go to John 12:32: **"And I, if I be lifted up from the earth, will draw all men unto me."** Go to 2 Corinthians chapter 6 – Scripture with Scripture – 2 Corinthians chapter 6 – make it 5, 2 Corinthians 5:19: **"To wit, that God was in Christ, reconciling the world unto himself, not imputing their trespasses unto them; and hath committed unto us the word of reconciliation."** Look at 20: **"We pray you in Christ's** stead, be ye reconciled to God." Look at 6:2: "Behold, now is the accepted time; behold, now is the day of salvation."

So quite simply, the Lord has drawn all men unto Himself, and He's now calling on men to repent, according to Acts 17, and believe the Gospel. So something very similar is found in the Garden of Eden. He's calling Adam; He's calling him to repentance. That's what's going on here. He knows where he is, of course, but He wants to see what Adam's going to say.

VERSES 10-11: **"And he said, I heard thy voice in the garden, and I was afraid, because I was naked; and I hid myself. And he said, Who told thee that thou wast naked? Hast thou eaten of the tree, whereof I commanded thee that thou shouldest not eat?"**

Now, here, again, is a picture of the Lord wanting a confession. And look at verse 12: **"And the man said, The woman whom thou gavest to be with me, she gave me of the tree, and I did eat."**

That's Adam's first mistake. He doesn't take responsibility; he blames the Lord and he blames the woman that He gave to Adam.

VERSE 13: **"And the LORD God said unto the woman, What is this that thou hast done? And the woman said, The serpent beguiled me, and I did eat."**

Now, both occasions here, they failed to confess their sin, and she passes the buck to the serpent.

VERSE 14: **"And the LORD God said unto the serpent, Because thou hast done this, thou art cursed above all cattle, and above every beast of the field; upon thy belly shalt thou go, and dust shalt thou eat all the days of thy life:"**

Now, here you find the devil in the person of the serpent punished, and he's going to slither on his belly all the days of his life. Snakes are pretty gruesome to look at at the best of times, and it never amazes me the amount of so-called Christians that are celebrities – I'm thinking of Alice Cooper. He comes to mind. This man claims to be born again, and yet he's happy to dangle snakes around and even mocks the account of Genesis chapter 3.

And in Mark 16 – I just want to look at this quickly – it says in Mark 16:18, "They shall take up serpents; and if they drink any deadly thing, it shall not hurt them." Now, of course, Paul didn't actually pick up a serpent as such. A serpent bit him, and as he moved his hand, it obviously was still stuck to his hand. But this other part, drink any deadly thing, it won't hurt them, no. This latter part of verse 18 is never cited by Pentecostals. And there have been accounts over the years of certain groups in parts of West Virginia and America who are messing around with snakes and have actually been killed by snakes, but you very rarely find them drinking any poison.

VERSE 15: "And I will put enmity between thee and the woman" – the woman here would be not only Eve but Israel also, and, of course, the devil has always been buffeting Israel – **"and between thy seed and her seed** – of course, Israel's seed ultimately will be the Lord Jesus Christ, and the seed, of course, here is a reference to not only the devil but his minions and all of the antichrist characters that have gone down through history – **"it shall bruise thy head, and thou shalt bruise his heel."**

Romans 16 speaks about the devil shortly being crushed, and this battle has gone on since creation. Satan thought he had destroyed Christ on the cross, which, of course, he hadn't done. The Lord was victorious. And the devil is going around like a roaring lion seeking to devour whom he may.

VERSE 16: "Unto the woman he said, I will greatly multiply thy sorrow and thy conception; in sorrow thou shalt bring forth children; and thy desire shall be to thy husband, and he shall rule over thee."

A picture of that in the New Testament would be a man and a woman both saved, and the husband would be the head of the family like the Father is the head of the Son. It doesn't mean that the husband treats his wife inferior or in a sort of second-class role. It's just that there has to be a head of every institution, if you will. There's a head of the government in the UK; there's a head of a company, and there's a head of the family, and there's a head in every aspect of life. It's pretty common and it hasn't died out even in this post-modern world that we live in.

VERSE 17: "And unto Adam he said, Because thou hast hearkened unto the voice of thy wife, and hast eaten of the tree, of which I commanded thee, saying, Thou shalt not eat of it: cursed is the ground for thy sake; in sorrow shalt thou eat of it all the days of thy life;"

This was a wilful rebellion. It wasn't just a mistake that he made. He rebelled by disobeying the Lord, and when the Lord confronted him, he didn't confess, he didn't repent; he passed the buck. So because of his wilful rebellion, the Lord is going to punish him all the days of his life, and because of this, everybody that's come from Adam has to work for a living. And a lot of people in the UK are doing two or three jobs just to make ends meet.

VERSES 18-19: "Thorns also and thistles shall it bring forth to thee; and thou shalt eat the herb of the field; In the sweat of thy face shalt thou eat bread, till thou return unto the ground; for out of it wast thou taken: for dust thou art, and unto dust shalt thou return."

Now, some people take this to be that there's no afterlife, but all He's saying is that you came from dust and you're going to go back to dust and await the resurrection.

VERSE 20: "And Adam called his wife's name Eve; because she was the mother of all living."

Now, again, interesting that he has the right even post fall to name his wife Eve, and she's the mother of all living.

I just want to add a quick footnote here. Go to Luke chapter 1:28: **"And the angel came in unto her, and said, Hail, thou that art highly favoured, the Lord is with thee: blessed art thou among women."** Of course, that's a reference to Mary, the mother of the Lord Jesus Christ. So she's blessed among women, and here Eve is called the mother of all living. Now, go to Judges 5:24: **"Blessed above women shall Jael the wife of Heber the Kenite be, blessed shall she be above women in the tent."** So just a small point, and yet a very significant point to flag up. Mary is called blessed <u>among</u> women, and she certainly was. The wife of Jael is blessed <u>above</u> women, and in Genesis 3 Eve is the mother of all living. So you need to put all these verses together to get a correct understanding of not only Mary in the New Testament but also Eve in the Old Testament, because if you just use a couple of verses or just one verse, you can fall into the trap of Mariolatry, which is endemic in Roman Catholicism. In fact, I'm going to show you one other point. It's very important to get these things cleared up. Go to Acts chapter 1. The Catholic church says that Mary is the Queen of Heaven. Look at Acts chapter 1 verse 13: **"And when they were come in, they went up into an upper room, where abode both Peter, and James, and John, and Andrew, Philip, and Thomas, Bartholomew, and Matthew, James the son of Alphaeus, and Simon Zelotes, and Judas the brother of James."** Look at 14: **"These all continued with one accord in prayer and supplication, with the women, and Mary the mother of Jesus,** and with his brethren." She's listed in 13th place. What's she doing in 13th place? If she's the Queen of Heaven and you can pray to her to have your prayers interceded, why is she listed in 13th place? And after this bit of Scripture, we never hear from Mary again. So just a brief footnote to show you.

VERSE 21: "Unto Adam also and to his wife did the LORD God make coats of skins, and clothed them."

Again, that's a reference quite possibly to some kind of imputed righteousness. The Lord doesn't look at sinners as they are. They have to have a covering; otherwise, they are consumed. And we are abhorrent in our own natural state to be in communion with the Lord. So this quite possibly is a picture of a righteousness given to them, which is found in the New Testament through Christ's imputed righteousness.

VERSE 22: "And the LORD God said, Behold, the man is become as one of us, to know good and evil: and now, lest he put forth his hand, and take also of the tree of life, and eat, and live for ever:

And here you see the problem that goes with verse 5 of chapter 3, and the devil says you'll be as gods knowing good and evil, and here the Lord is saying you'll be like us to know good from evil. And, of course, that reference to **"us"** is to the triune God. To stop Adam taking of the tree, which, as you know, is a reference to eternal life – the Old Testament speaks of Eden lost; the New Testament speaks of Eden restored, and had he taken of the Tree of Life, he would have lived forever on the earth like a vagabond, a bit like Cain that we'll get to in a minute. So the Lord stops that happening, and 24 explains what He does. But look at 23:

VERSES 23-24: "Therefore the LORD God sent him forth from the garden of Eden, to till the ground from whence he was taken. So he drove out the man; and he placed at the east of the garden of

Eden Cherubims, and a flaming sword which turned every way, to keep the way of the tree of life."

It's interesting that verse 1 of Genesis 3 opens with a cherub because Satan is a cherub, and it closes with two cherubs keeping Adam out of the Garden of Eden. And one can only wonder what the world would have been like had Adam and Eve not sinned. Death wouldn't have come; Jesus wouldn't have had to leave Heaven and die for the sins of the world. Adam and Eve would have gone on to produce children, which would have produced children, and there would have been a nice fairytale ending. But, of course, it wasn't to be. Satan had already fallen, and it wasn't long before he deceived the first parents, and since then, the whole world has gone into absolute meltdown. But although that was the case, God knew in eternity past this would happen. Jesus Christ offered, volunteered to die for the sins of the world to appease the Lord's mercy, the Lord's holiness, the Lord's love and desire for justice; and it's obvious, really – isn't it? – that if you sin against God, only God Himself can forgive you.

Okay. Just before we get on to the fourth chapter, I want to add a quick footnote which, I think, may be important and of interest to you. In Genesis 2:17, the Scripture says **"for in the day that thou eatest thereof thou shalt surely die."** Here the Lord is speaking to Adam. It's a very clear and unequivocal statement that if he was to eat of the tree of the knowledge and good and evil, he would surely die. And by chapter 3 verse 3, Eve speaks to the serpent and she says, **"Ye shall not eat of it, neither shall ye touch it, lest ye die"** – quite a difference between **"lest ye die"** to **"surely die."** And I was thinking about this last night, and 1 Samuel chapter 3 verse 1 came to my mind, and I thought a very similar sort of set up: **"And the child Samuel ministered unto the LORD before Eli. And the word of the LORD was precious in those days; there was no open vision. And it came to pass at that time, when Eli was laid down in his place, and his eyes began to wax dim, that he** could not see; And ere the lamp of God went out in the temple of the LORD, where the ark of God was, and Samuel was laid down to sleep; That the LORD called Samuel: and he answered, Here am I. And he ran unto Eli, and said, Here am I; for thou calledst me. And he said, I called not; lie down again. And he went and lay down. And the LORD called yet again, Samuel. And Samuel arose and went to Eli, and said, Here am I; for thou didst call me. And he answered, I called not, my son; lie down again. Now Samuel did not yet know the LORD, neither was the word of the LORD yet revealed unto him. And the LORD called Samuel again the third time. And he arose and went to Eli, and said, Here am I; for thou didst call me. And Eli perceived that the LORD had called the child" (vv. 1-8.) Now look at verse 9: "Therefore Eli said unto Samuel, Go, lie down: and it shall be, if he call thee, that thou shalt say, Speak, LORD; for thy servant heareth. So Samuel went and lay down in his place. And the LORD came, and stood, and called as at other times, Samuel, Samuel. Then Samuel answered, Speak; for thy servant heareth" (vv.9-10.)

Now, do you notice that this is a young child, Samuel, similar mentality to Adam and Eve, and when he gets to speak to the Lord, he doesn't call Him LORD. He was told in verse 9 to say **"Speak, LORD,"** and all he says here is, **"Speak; for thy servant heareth."** It's a small omittance, but it's an important omittance, and the reason I've shown you this bit of Scripture is because I think that Adam and Eve, although they had dominion, although they were able to name the animals, talk to the animals – especially Adam – I still retain the position that Eve, especially, was quite childlike, and that, of course, is innocency. It's great that children are innocent from all of the fallen and sinful and cynics and this wicked, depraved society which is all around us. But here the young child Samuel doesn't repeat word-for-word what he was told by the older Eli. And I think if you were to pull all this together, I think back in the Garden that Eve was not only seduced by the serpent, but she was probably fearful of him and certainly intimidated; and although she did omit the words from verse 17 of chapter 2, I think when we put it altogether and we look at the reaction from 3:12 and 3:13 and 3:14, we see in reality that these two people, Adam and Eve, were childlike. So just a footnote to add, and let me know your thoughts on that.

CHAPTER 4

VERSE 1: "And Adam knew Eve his wife; and she conceived, and bare Cain, and said, I have gotten a man from the LORD."

Genesis 2, the Lord told Adam and Eve to replenish the earth, to bring forth their seed, to start the human race. In Genesis chapter 3:20 Eve is called **"the mother of all living."** So it should be crystal clear, I hope, that this expression "knew his wife" is a metaphor for sexual intercourse. And when we go to Matthew chapter 1 – Scripture with Scripture – Matthew chapter 1, look at verse 24: **"Then Joseph being raised from sleep did as the angel of the Lord had bidden him, and took unto him his wife: And knew her not till she had brought forth her firstborn son: and he called his name JESUS"** (vv. 24-25.) Now, it's really clear when you read Genesis 4, Matthew 1 – and I'll show you one more in a minute – when you read these verses together that it is always referring to sexual intercourse, and it says here that he didn't know her until she brought forth her firstborn son. Now, as you know, the Catholic church doesn't like the idea of Mary, their Queen of Heaven, having other children. In fact, go to Mark 6. Now, the Muslims call Jesus the son of Mary, a term which only occurs once in the word of God in Mark 6. He's called the Son of man 80 times and the Son of God 40 times directly and indirectly. If you go to Mark 6 verse 3: **"Is not this the carpenter, the son of Mary, the brother of James, and Joses, and of Juda, and Simon? and are not his sisters here with us? And they were offended at him."** So here you find that Christ had four brothers and at least two sisters. The sisters are spoken of as plural, so at least two sisters, and they are never named in Scripture, which isn't unusual. The women aren't always named in the genealogies in the Old

Testament either, which shows me that Mark was a Jew – and someone said he may not have been, but, nonetheless, the style here is Jewish through and through.

Now, the reason I just wanted to show you this is to try and expound a bit more that Mary wasn't a perpetual virgin, and, of course, in Catholic circles that is paramount because they don't like the idea, as I say, of the Queen of Heaven having – what? – five, six, seven children. And that doesn't negate the fact that she was still holy, she was set apart to give birth to the Lord Jesus Christ, but we know through medical terms that the placenta, the mother's placenta, the place obviously where the child is borne in the mother's womb, the placenta doesn't mix with the child's blood. It's the father's blood, never the mother's blood. And for those that know a bit of medicine, you will hopefully affirm what I've just said. But Mary was a sinner; she was born in sin, and even the early church fathers and leaders even – I think it was Leo the Great and Gregory the Great – these lovely terms they give themselves – even they said that she was a sinner. And Paul says all have sinned and come short of the glory of God (Rom. 3:23.)

Also, again, the word of God has to be our final authority. Let's just say for argument's sake that Mary had the Lord and He was her first and only born child. She's still married to Joseph. Joseph has needs, and you would have thought that she would have had needs too. Go to 1 Corinthians chapter 7. Look at verse 3: **"Let the husband render unto the wife due benevolence: and likewise also the wife unto the husband. The wife hath not power of her own body, but the husband: and likewise also the husband hath not power of his own body, but the wife"** (vv. 3-4.) Look at 5: **"Defraud ye not one the other, except it be with consent for a time, that ye may give yourselves to fasting and prayer; and come together again, that Satan tempt you not for your incontinency"** – in other words, you can separate through prayer and fasting, abstinence from intercourse, but after a time, you've got to come back together and keep the marriage bed alive. Why? Well, of course, if you don't have regular intercourse in marriage, then one or the other may stray, and it causes all sorts of problems. Of course, that doesn't make it mandatory. I mean, there are some people in marriages who are impotent and there are some in marriages who don't want to have that sexual union, and that's normally due to physical reasons. But here the apostle Paul has it in mind that if you're a healthy, average couple, sexual intercourse is going to be necessary to keep the marriage strong.

Just one other Scripture quickly. Go to 1 Timothy. I've heard Catholics say – this will be a side point, by the way, but I've heard Catholics say that when Peter, their first pope – allegedly – became the first pope, that he left his wife. And I don't think that's a generally held view in Catholic circles. I wasn't taught that as a Catholic, but it has been spoken about throughout the years. And in 1 Timothy 5:8 Paul says: **"But if any provide not for his own, and specially for those of his own house, he hath denied the faith, and is worse than an infidel."** So that would put Peter in a very awkward position and also Joseph. Joseph would have had obligations to support Mary and their seven children. Of course, Jesus wasn't Joseph's child; the Holy Ghost came upon Mary and she gave birth. Jesus Christ is the sinless Son of God.

Just one other quick thing to show you which you may find interesting. When you go through the Old Testament, all of the kings and prophets are all types of Christ. Go to 1 Samuel chapter 2:26: **"And the child Samuel grew on, and was in favour both with the LORD, and also with men."** There's a type of Christ. There's your mediator between God and man, the man Christ Jesus from 1 Timothy 2:5. But here Samuel is a type of Christ. Look at 25: **"If one man sin against another, the judge shall judge him: but if a man sin against the LORD, who shall intreat for him?"** Time and time we go through the word of God and you get progressive revelation. I mean, in the

Old Testament Abraham didn't know God's name was Jehovah but Moses did. And there is this theme, especially in the book of Job: How can man be justified with God? How can man be exonerated? How can a holy God look at man? And throughout the whole of the Old Testament that is echoed time and time again. Of course, in the New Testament Jesus Christ, the Lamb of God, comes on the earth and He is completely God. There are some people who call themselves Christians and they would say in conservative circles that Jesus was a good man, He was commissioned by the Lord but He wasn't God. And, of course, that falls flat on its face because if you sin against God, only God Himself can exonerate you, and we've talked about that on other videos.

But here you see Samuel as a young mediator. And I'll show you one other quick point, and then we'll get back to Genesis. Look at 1 Samuel 2:21: **"And the LORD visited Hannah, so that she conceived, and bare three sons and two daughters. And the child Samuel grew before the LORD"** – very similar between Mary and Hannah. Mary has five sons, including Christ, and at least two daughters.

And just one final point if you're still not convinced of this expression "knowing" the wife, henceforth, bringing forth children. First Samuel 1:19: **"And they rose up in the morning early, and worshipped before the LORD, and returned, and came to their house to Ramah: and Elkanah knew Hannah his wife; and the LORD remembered her"**; 20, **"Wherefore it came to pass, when the time was come about after Hannah had conceived, that she bare a son, and called his name Samuel."** So you can see quite clearly – not that you needed to, but just in case there were some that were still unsure – that when you "know" somebody in the Bible, that is a reference, a discreet reference to sexual intercourse.

Okay. Go back to Genesis 4:2:

VERSE 2: "And she" – Eve – **"again bare his brother Abel. And Abel was a keeper of sheep, but Cain was a tiller of the ground."**

The Lord Jesus Christ is called the Good Shepherd, and He said my sheep hear my voice and they follow me (Jn. 10:27.) Matthew 25, the Lord Jesus Christ has His sheep and the goats, and the sheep are the saved; they are the redeemed; they are the ones that appropriated the atonement; they received the forgiveness of sins, and the goats are those that did not receive the forgiveness of the Lord. And it's quite clear – in fact, let's go to Matthew 25 quickly. Forgive the jumping around, but these videos are not scripted. I just speak as I go through, and hopefully you can keep up with me. Matthew 25:46: **"And these shall go away into everlasting punishment: but the righteous into life eternal."** Somebody was a little upset with my video "Alive in Hell," I think it was – I've done several videos on Hell – and the comment was something like, "How can you teach that unsaved people have everlasting life?" Well, the Bible says they go into everlasting punishment, and when did "everlasting" ever not mean without end? So it is absolutely true that if you're not saved, you still get everlasting life, but not in Heaven, not with the Lord. You will live forever. Of course, that is the second death. Hell and Hades – whatever you want to call it – are cast alive into the lake of fire. And I've tried to make the case in other videos that the first death is physical, literal – there's talking, there's speaking. Luke 16 is not a parable, and you go to any Bible, any Scripture and look up Luke 16 verse 19 to 31 and you will not find the word "parable" written in there.

People don't like this doctrine of Hell; they don't like the idea that there is a consciousness when you go to sleep, and they don't like it because obviously it's pricking their conscience. And we know that when our body dies, almost straightaway the weight of the body decreases. It doesn't happen with animals but it happens with humans. And some people have taken that to be proof that the soul departs the minute you die. And you don't need to be a genius to work out where the soul has gone if you're a Bible-believing Christian – Heaven if you're saved; Hell if you're lost. I might come back to that in a minute.

Back to Genesis 4:2: "And she" – Eve – **"again bare his brother Abel. And Abel was a keeper of sheep, but Cain was a tiller of the ground."** Abel is a type of Christ on at least two accounts. The first account, he's a keeper of sheep. Psalm 23, the word of God says, **"The LORD is my shepherd."** LORD is uppercase. It refers to God. John chapter 10, Jesus said, **"I am the good shepherd"** (v. 14.) Those two verses quite clearly and unequivocally, I put to you, affirm the deity of Christ. The second account is that Abel is soon to be put to death prematurely, and he's put to death by his own brother. Now, when we look at the death of Christ, we have to keep several things in mind – first of all that Jesus is God, and man cannot force God's hand. The word of God says that Christ had power to lay His life down and to take it up again. He said to Pilate, You have no authority, you have no power over me except it were given to you. He humbled Himself, took on the nature of a man, and lay His life down for the sins of the world. So keep that in mind.

Go to Matthew 27 verse 25: **"Then answered all the people"** – these are the Jews, the unbelieving Jews – **"and said, his blood be on us, and on our children."** So they have just cursed themselves. They've called for the precious blood of Christ to not only be put on them but on their children. And hasn't history shown that to be so? Go to 1 Thessalonians – Scripture with Scripture – 1 Thessalonians chapter 2 verse 14: **"For ye, brethren, became followers of the churches of God which in Judaea are in Christ Jesus: for ye also have suffered like things of your own countrymen, even as they have of the Jews: Who both killed the Lord Jesus, and their own prophets, and have persecuted us; and they please not God, and are contrary to all men: Forbidding us to speak to the Gentiles that they might be saved, to fill up their sins alway: for the wrath is come upon them to** the uttermost" (vv. 14-16.) Okay. So you have a very strong, powerful group of unbelieving Jews that were prophesied back in Isaiah and Jeremiah that would not only refuse to receive the Lord but would later put Him to death.

Go to Matthew 21:43: **"Therefore say I unto you, The kingdom of God shall be taken from you, and given to a nation bringing forth the fruits thereof. And whosoever shall fall on this stone shall be broken: but on whomsoever it shall fall, it will grind him to powder"** (vv. 43-44.) **So Matthew 21:43 says the Kingdom has been taken from the Jews and given to a nation. The apostle Peter said we are a peculiar people. So nation and people are synonymous, normally means "the peoples."**

So the Kingdom was taken from the Jews, and normally those that hold to Replacement Theology will use that bit of Scripture to show that the church has replaced the Jews, which is partially correct. For the church age at least, we have replaced Israel. Go to Romans 11:28: **"As concerning the gospel, they are enemies for your sakes: but as touching the election, they are beloved for the fathers' sakes. For the gifts and calling of God are without repentance"** (vv. 28-29). So Paul is quite clear to say that the Jews, as of his generation, as of his day, as of his time were enemies of the church. They put the Lord to death; they killed Stephen, and Jesus said they even killed the prophets going back to the Old Testament, and the judgment fell on that generation. So I have no problem teaching that the Jews put the Lord Jesus Christ to death. Some of you would say that's not politically correct. Well, so be it. This isn't a politically correct ministry. We are Bible-believing Christians, and we believe the whole Bible, and, where possible, we present it in its entirety.

Go back to Genesis chapter 4 verse 3: **"And in process of time it came to pass, that Cain brought of the fruit of the ground an offering unto the LORD."**

Do you realise that in eternity, for an unsaved man or woman nothing comes to pass? Do you realise that the man in Luke 16, verses 19 to 31, is still in the ground? When Christ died, He went into the ground and He scooped up the righteous, took them to glory, but He left the wicked dead still in Hell, which is the first death, and they will be in Hell until the Great White Throne. If the Rapture came tomorrow, you'd have the seven-year tribulation period, if that was to follow the Rapture – and it will, I'm sure – then you have a thousand year reign where Jesus Christ reigns on the earth, and all of the unsaved dead stay in the ground until the end of the thousand years. That man in Luke 16 is still in Hell. Nothing comes to pass in Hell. The Scripture says, **"it came to pass, that Cain brought of the fruit of the ground an offering unto the LORD."** So his intention here is partially right. Look at verse 4:

VERSES 4-5: "And Abel, he also brought of the firstlings of his flock and of the fat thereof. And the LORD had respect unto Abel and to his offering: But unto Cain and to his offering he had not respect. And Cain was very wroth, and his countenance fell."

Abel, once again, is a type of Christ. Christ's offering was perfect, without blemish. God received it, totally appeased His holiness and His wrath, and everything was dealt with through Christ's atonement. The unbelieving Jews didn't receive that; they rejected it, and they continued going to the Temple, and the Lord gave them 40 years before He destroyed the Temple. Again, Cain is a type of the unbelieving Jew, and he's ultimately a type of the Antichrist. God has respect to Abel's sacrifice, not to Cain's. Again, that's quite clear.

Verse 5, **"But unto Cain and to his offering he had not respect. And Cain was very wroth, and his countenance fell."** Again, the Jews despised Christ; they said, "We won't have this man to reign over us. If the people believe on Him, the Romans will come, take away our kingdom, and we will be just like everybody else" – very similar language here.

VERSE 6: "And the LORD said unto Cain, Why art thou wroth? and why is thy countenance fallen?"

Time and time again the Lord will reason with men and He'll give men the chance to confess their sin and forsake it.

VERSE 7: "If thou doest well, shalt thou not be accepted? and if thou doest not well, sin lieth at the door. And unto thee shall be his desire, and thou shalt rule over him."

Cain is the oldest and he's going to have the ability to reign over his younger brother Abel, as all firstborns did in biblical times. And, of course, the Lord is giving Cain the chance to come clean. He's pleading with Cain. It says in Isaiah 1, **"Come now, and let us reason together, saith the LORD"** (v. 18.) There's always that calling; there's always that desire that God wants to be reconciled to sinful people, but men love darkness rather than light.

VERSE 8: "And Cain talked with Abel his brother: and it came to pass, when they were in the field, that Cain rose up against Abel his brother, and slew him."

Again, the first murder has been recorded here in Scripture. And somebody said, "I don't like the Bible; it's a very bloody, it's a very rough book." The Bible is a very honest book, and it's a reflection of all of humankind. And here you have a brother killing his other brother. Again, it's a type of Christ. Abel was a good man; his sacrifice was received of the Lord. And his brother is wicked; he's flawed; he kills his brother – and very picturesque, very typical of a type of Old Testament saint. He's going to be a type of Christ.

VERSE 9: "And the LORD said unto Cain, Where is Abel thy brother? And he said, I know not: Am I my brother's keeper?"

Cain is a liar; he's a murderer, and he's also quick with his tongue – sarcastic. People say that original sin isn't biblical. Well, what do you do with verse 9? He's almost citing his father Adam. Adam sinned; God confronted him; he doesn't confess. The Lord always gives man a chance to repent, a chance to come clean, and men throw it back in God's face. This is original sin: (a) original sin is to know the difference between good and evil and (b) it's to follow through on the evil and do that which the Lord hates, that which is abhorrent to the Lord. And it says here, **"Am I my brother's keeper?"** – very similar language to Adam when he blames Eve for his downfall and he puts it back on the Lord. He doesn't take responsibility for his own actions – again, very much like a wayward child.

VERSE 10: "And he said, What hast thou done? the voice of thy brother's blood crieth unto me from the ground."

This is the third time that the Lord has given Cain the chance to come clean. There's nothing in this Scripture to suggest that God hardened Cain's heart to do what he did, to cause his brother's murder. This came from the heart of Cain. It's jealousy; it's pride. Satan fell through pride, and Cain is a child of the devil. And you're going to see this throughout the whole of the Bible – these two lines. Again, it goes back to Genesis 3. The seed of Eve is going to be in conflict with the seed of the devil.

VERSE 11: "And now art thou cursed from the earth, which hath opened her mouth to receive thy brother's blood from thy hand;"

A man reaps what he sows.

VERSE 12: "When thou tillest the ground, it shall not henceforth yield unto thee her strength; a fugitive and a vagabond shalt thou be in the earth."

The wages (the price, penalty) of sin is death.

VERSE 13: "And Cain said unto the LORD, My punishment is greater than I can bear."

Go to Lamentations. When God judges the unsaved dead, according to Lamentations 3:39, **"Wherefore doth a living man complain, a man for the punishment of his sins?"** When God judges the world, the unsaved, wicked, depraved dead man will have nothing to say. He cannot complain for his sins. If you died an adulterer, you died a fornicator, if you died a drunkard – whatever you were into – you will stand before God and you will give an account of yourself to Him. Nobody forced you to be an alcoholic; nobody forced you to be an adulterer or a fornicator or whatever it was that ultimately destroyed you. All those sins that you died in, all those options, those opportunities, all those decisions that you did which ultimately caused you to reject Christ, you will have to give an account of yourself. Lamentations makes it quite clear that you are going to give an account of yourself, and you are your own worst enemy when it comes to the judgment. Cain here is crying out to the Lord. He knows that he's done wrong.

VERSE 14: "Behold, thou hast driven me out this day from the face of the earth; and from thy face shall I be hid; and I shall be a fugitive and a vagabond in the earth; and it shall come to pass, that every one that findeth me shall slay me."

Man has that conscience. I've seen these documentaries normally put out by crime experts, and they will do a profile on a serial killer, and they'll say this party and that party didn't have a conscience. That is questionable. I would say that the jury is out on that. Paul does say that people can be given over to a debased mind and their conscience is seared with a hot iron, but the Bible says that man has a conscience and he suppresses the truth in unrighteousness. Here we have the murder of Cain here, and he's crying out to the Lord, and yet remarkably the Lord does give him grace.

VERSE 15: "And the LORD said unto him, Therefore whosoever slayeth Cain, vengeance shall be taken on him sevenfold." Now, we are before the law here. Had this occurred during the law, he would have been put to death. This wasn't manslaughter, which is different to murder; this was premeditated murder, and yet the Lord shows him grace. **"And the LORD set a mark upon Cain, lest any finding him should kill him."**

Whatever that mark was, it was quite clear that the Lord didn't want this man to be executed for his crime. He wants him to continue on. And, of course, from Cain came more people.

VERSES 16-17: "And Cain went out from the presence of the LORD" – That is a profound statement. That means, really, that from this moment on, Cain had no more dealings with God – **"and dwelt in the land of Nod, on the east of Eden. And Cain knew his wife"** – which would be his sister, of course – **"and she conceived, and bare Enoch: and he builded a city, and called the name of the city, after the name of his son, Enoch."**

His wife here, of course, is his sister. Adam and Eve had many children. This was before the fall. This was before the problem of incest. There was no genetic deformity here. And from Adam to Abraham, there's a period of about 2,000 years. So that, of course, is why and how Adam and Eve were able to produce hundreds of children, which produced other children. And, of course, the longevity was hundreds of years. This, of course, is before the flood of Noah, and bit by bit as we go through the Old Testament, the longevity drops off. In the Millennium, it will return. If you die a hundred years old, that will be considered an infant in the Millennium.

VERSES 18, 19, 20, children are born to the line of Cain through Enoch. And look at 21:

VERSE 21: "And his brother's name was Jubal: he was the father of all such as handle the harp and organ."

This is interesting. This is the first reference to music in Genesis. The book of Job says the sons of God sang for God's glory, and we know that Lucifer before he fell was also built with some kind of instrument which gave the Lord some kind of worship. The book of Revelation says that the saved worship the Lord and they praise Him every day. But this here is a reference to a man, unfortunately in the line of Cain, and he is the father of the harp and organ. Look at 23:

VERSE 22: "And Zillah, she also bare Tubalcain, an instructer of every artificer in brass and iron: and the sister of Tubalcain was Naamah."

VERSE 23: "And Lamech said unto his wives, Adah and Zillah, Hear my voice; ye wives of Lamech, hearken unto my speech: for I have slain a man to my wounding, and a young man to my hurt."

Interesting that we find the first account of polygamy. It was practiced throughout the Old Testament. All of the kings had multiple wives. I think one of the few exceptions in the Old Testament was Moses. I think he only had Zipporah, his only wife. But throughout the Old Testament, polygamy is very prolific, and, of course, in the New Testament it is completely unheard of. Here you find a man, Lamech, who has slain a man to his wounding. Look at 24:

VERSE 24: "If Cain shall be avenged sevenfold, truly Lamech seventy and sevenfold."

Clearly he knows that justice will follow him and ultimately he will be put to death for his sin. I want to say just one thing while I'm on this part of Scripture that when we get to the later parts of the Old Testament, if you take a life, you lose a life, you forfeit your own life. Jesus Christ upheld that in the Gospel of – I think it was Luke. He said that he that liveth by the sword shall die by the sword, and Paul says in Romans 13 that he that takes the sword doesn't take it in vain. Capital punishment has always been a theme, not only in the Bible but in civilised society. However, back in the 1960s a man called Pierrepoint, who was the hangman in the UK for many, many years, was the last of the hangmen in the UK. And it was, I think, mid 60s that the British government abolished the death penalty, and since then, murder has gone up tenfold in the UK. Most people that have committed a crime of murder in the UK would be quite happy to be put to death. I won't name any particular criminals because it's not necessary, but there have been recent events in the news of well-known people who have committed murder that have tried to commit suicide to escape their sin, their guilt, and their shame. That will stay with you until you die. If you're not born again, that hangs over you.

But this man here Lamech and Cain his great grandfather would normally have been put to death, but the Lord has suspended that sentence, and we have nothing more from Scripture to suggest what happened to them. It's quite likely, as I say, that they probably lived out their life not saved, of course, and they were awaiting their death. Ten in ten people will die, and judgment will come to them.

VERSE 25: "And Adam knew his wife again; and she bare a son, and called his name Seth: For God, said she, hath appointed me another seed instead of Abel, whom Cain slew."

Similar language to the New Testament. Christ is put to death, and His seed, which, of course, is the church, continues on in His absence. Of course, the church becomes sons of God, according to 1 John 3, but we don't become deity; we don't become divinity. That is the mistake that the Mormons make.

VERSE 26: "And to Seth, to him also there was born a son; and he called his name Enos: then began men to call upon the name of the LORD."

Very, very interesting. Romans 10 says whosoever calleth on the name of the Lord shall be saved (Rom 10:13.)

So we started with the birth of two boys. We finish with one of their murders. We finish with the grandson of Cain also with blood on his hands, and yet also with that bloodshed came the birth of Seth, who is a type of Christ, and Jesus Christ will come through the line of Seth. And Seth had a son called Enos, and through Enos, that line starts the practice, the perpetual practice of calling on the name of the Lord.

CHAPTER 5

VERSES 1-2: "This is the book of the generations of Adam. In the day that God created man, in the likeness of God made he him; Male and female created he them; and blessed them, and called their name Adam, in the day when they were created."

Okay. Let's look at this in reverse order. Verse 2, **"Male and female created he them; and blessed them, and called their name Adam."** A girl is born and she takes her father's name. She will grow up, meet a boy of her dreams, marry him and take his name. Children will be born, and they will take their father's name. That isn't chauvinism; that is a biblical fact. This was written 1500 BC going back even further than that, and yet here we are in the 21st century some 6,000 years on from this account of Genesis chapter 5, give or take some years here and there, and yet every civilised nation anywhere on the planet still practices this part of Scripture. Whether they realise it or not is irrelevant. The Lord sets the pace, and the world follows too – very, very interesting.

Look at verse 1: **"This is the book of the generations of Adam."** Generations is spoken of in plural. Adam was the first man, and, of course, from Adam came the human race. And when you go through the whole of the fifth chapter, which I won't do due to a time limit, but when you go through the fifth chapter, many of his sons and their sons and their daughters are very clearly found throughout the Scripture. There aren't many religions from antiquity that have a record such as this.

Go to Matthew chapter 1. Adam is the first man; Jesus is the second man. Matthew 1:1: **"The book of the generation of Jesus Christ, the**

son of David, the son of Abraham." I remember watching a video lecture some time ago of David Icke, and he was going through Matthew's Gospel. Icke, for those that don't know, isn't a Christian. He's into the new age, and he is anti-Christian. In fact, he's probably as far from being a Bible-believing Christian is to the Chinese Premier. He is anti-Scripture, and he's also a very ignorant man. And I say that not to malign him but to reflect the truth. The Bible says that the unlearned and the ignorant people twist the Scripture to their own damnation. And he was going through Matthew's Gospel chapter 1, and he thought it was rather amusing that this first book in the New Testament would begin with a genealogy. In fact, if you add up all these people here, you get the number 42, and 42 is an interesting number because Jesus was on the earth for 42 months, give or take a few months here or there, but about 42 months, and the Antichrist will be on the earth for 42 months. Some people may think that's a coincidence, but maybe it is, and maybe it's not. But Icke didn't understand that Matthew was a Jew; he's writing to the Jews, and he's doing what all Jews would expect him to do – he's showing Christ's lineage; he's showing his genealogy going right back to Abraham, whereas Luke is tracing Him right back to Adam. So because of ignorance that is found in a lot of these anti-Christian circles, these people think they can refute and dismiss the Bible when, in reality, they're simply showing their ignorance.

I was talking to a Rabbi on the street, and you get some very interesting conversations on the street. In fact, I would put to you that most Christians that don't do any sort of street ministry will never meet people from the real world.

Just a quick footnote before I get back to the Rabbi. I was talking to a church leader quite recently who was telling me that he had been trying to encourage some of his colleagues to go out onto the streets and do some open-air work, and he put it to me that a lot of his friends were quite happy and content to mix with Christians and never go into the real world. And I thought how sad it was that those that are in organised religion are content to be cocooned with other Christians, whereas the Scripture says we are to go into all the world and preach the Gospel and be ready in season and out of season to give a defence of the faith that is in us. And the Scripture does say that the common people gladly received Him. They were very happy to hear what He had to say. But it's tragic because a lot of these church people never actually mix with the world, and therefore they have no witness; they have no testimony.

But like I was saying, I was talking to this Rabbi on the street, and we had quite a good conversation. And I said to him that there were no original manuscripts for the Old Testament, and the same is true of the New Testament also. And he didn't like me saying that, and we had quite a debate on the manuscripts of the Bible. But he made an interesting point. He said to me that even if the case of the manuscripts was so, he said, "I have a father who had a father who had a father that can trace their lineage right back to Mount Sinai. They can go right back to Moses." And he's absolutely right. In fact, any Jew living anywhere in the world today can trace their lineage right back to Abraham. He was from the tribe of Levi, whichever way you wish to pronounce it, but he made a good point, a very valid point. Now, of course, that doesn't make him any more spiritual. That doesn't mean that he's any more religious, and he certainly isn't saved. Just because he's born a Jew doesn't mean that God will receive him. He too must be born again. But nonetheless, his comment about the Jews going right back to even Adam, really, is spot-on. In fact, they are the only religion, to the best of my knowledge, that have a very clear and almost unbroken line going right back to the first Jew.

And I'll just say this before I move on. The Catholic church makes quite a noise about having an unbroken line of popes going back to

Peter, and they believe they've had 265 popes. Now, I believe that line has been broken many times throughout the Dark Ages, and for 700 years the so-called chair of Peter wasn't only occupied by children and other dubious people, shall we say, but on several occasions you had more than one pope on the throne. But even if we were to accept the claim that the Catholics put forward for their unbroken line of popes, that doesn't make them any more spiritual; it doesn't give them any more level of credence. It simply means they are religious people with a long line. Even Hindus and Sikhs can claim a long line, but what does it prove? It proves nothing whatsoever. But for the Jews, something which is distinguished from other religions is an unbroken line, and I just thought it might be worth sharing that with you.

Okay. Let's go back to Genesis, Scripture with Scripture, Genesis chapter 5 verse 3: **"And Adam lived an hundred and thirty years, and begat a son in his own likeness, after his image; and called his name Seth:"**

There are some Christians that believe that when Adam sinned, he lost the image that he had been given from the Lord, and subsequently everybody who's born since Adam or since Seth, to be more precise, has the image of Seth. Now, I don't understand that logic. Paul speaks about us being in the similitude – another word for image – of God in 1 Corinthians, so I have no reason to doubt that we are all born in the image of God. And we certainly all have the problem of original sin. And, yes, I know the word "original sin" came from Augustine, but the doctrine, the theology behind the word "original sin" is very much scriptural. And I've already shown you that when Adam fell, he lied; he passed the blame over to his wife Eve; and when Cain killed his brother, he also tried to duck his responsibility and pass the buck back to the Lord. That is a picture of original sin. Original sin is to know the difference between good and evil and to choose evil, because man is born in sin; he's born in rebellion.

VERSES 4-5: "And the days of Adam after he had begotten Seth were eight hundred years: and he begat sons and daughters: And all the days that Adam lived were nine hundred and thirty years: and he died."

And that is all we have on the death of Adam. We cannot say for sure whether he was saved or lost. The church is split on this, and if you were to ask ten Christians, you would get a 50-50 response. We don't know, so it's best not to speculate. Look at 21-23: **"And Enoch lived sixty and five years, and begat Methuselah: And Enoch walked with God after he begat Methuselah three hundred years, and begat sons and daughters: And all the days of Enoch were three hundred sixty and five years:"**

Look at 24: **"And Enoch walked with God: and he was not; for God took him."**

This is the first reference to a rapture in the word of God. Here's a man who was living with the Lord, walking with the Lord, and one day the Lord took him. He never died. Go to John, John chapter 11. I just want to show you a New Testament picture of this – John 11:25: **"I am the resurrection, and the life: he that believeth in me, though he were dead, yet shall he live: And whosoever liveth and believeth in me shall never die"** (vv. 25-26.)

Okay. So if you are alive today and the Rapture came today, you wouldn't die; you would go up in the sky, up in the air, and, of course, as you are raptured, you get a new body at the same time. Flesh and blood cannot inherit the Kingdom of God, so God changes you in the twinkling of an eye. If you are dead and the Rapture occurs, then you get a new body, and up you go. And I believe John 11 is probably the easiest and quickest way to harmonise Genesis chapter 5 verse 24. Look at 29-32: **"And he called his name Noah, saying, This same shall comfort us concerning our work and toil of our hands, because of**

the ground which the LORD hath cursed. And Lamech lived after he begat Noah five hundred ninety and five years, and begat sons and daughters: And all the days of Lamech were seven hundred seventy and seven years: and he died. And Noah was five hundred years old: and Noah begat Shem, Ham, and Japheth."

As you can see, these men of old are still way up into the mid hundreds, but as you go through Scripture, the life span of man goes right down, and by the time you get to the New Testament, the average life span of a person living in Israel in the first century was about 70 years old. So John the apostle, who lived well into his 90s, was very much the exception and not the norm. But, of course, Noah is in the right line. He's in the line of Seth, and, of course, he's going to produce Shem, Ham, and Japheth, and from Shem we believe comes the Hebrews. So this is very much a righteous line. That doesn't mean everybody that was born in the line of Shem is going to be sinless. There's going to be a lot of pain, a lot of anguish, a lot of sin, which we'll get to in the later chapters of Genesis.

But as you can see from 24, we found the Rapture, a picture of a person who will never die and will always be with the Lord, and we find a picture of Noah, who is also a type of a Jew in the Tribulation, and he builds an ark and takes the Jews – now, this, again, is a picture of the Jews through the Tribulation – and they come out at the other end. But we'll look at that more in the next few chapters.

CHAPTER 6

———

VERSES 1-2: "And it came to pass, when men began to multiply on the face of the earth, and daughters were born unto them, That the sons of God saw the daughters of men that they were fair; and they took them wives of all which they chose."

Okay. There are two schools of thought as to who these sons of God are, and the first position and the most popular position, I should say, is that this is a reference to Adam's sons. And they will show you Luke chapter 3 verse 38, **"Which was a son of Enos, which was a son of Seth, which was the son of Adam, which was the son of God,"** and they show you this to affirm, they would have you believe, that sons of God can refer to humans, which, of course, it does. Go to 1 John 3:2: **"Beloved, now are we the sons of God,"** and I'll give you one more. Go to John, Gospel of John chapter 1 – and you know this very well, but I want to read it anyway. John 1:12: **"But as many as received him, to them gave he power to become the sons of God, even to them that believe on his name."** So those two Scriptures from the New Testament do show clearly that the expression "sons of God" can refer to human beings.

The second view is that this is a reference to angels. Go to the book of Job. Job is probably the oldest book in the Bible, and some people believe that Moses wrote the book of Job. Job chapter 1:6: **"Now there was a day when the sons of God came to present themselves before the LORD, and Satan came also among them"**; Chapter 2 verse 1: **"Again there was a day when the sons of God came to present themselves before the LORD, and Satan came also among them to present himself before the LORD."** Go to 38, chapter 38 verse 7: **"When the morning stars sang together, and all the sons of God**

shouted for joy?" So this expression **"morning stars"** – and Revelation speaks about the stars falling from Heaven – is a metaphor for angels. But here you have the morning stars in the same reference as the sons of God. So you have equal Scripture to affirm that the sons of God can either be human or they can be angelic, and the reality is that by chapter 6 of Genesis, these sons of God, I would put to you, are angelic. That's my position, and for many years it was the most popular position, but in recent years with Christianity going into decline, this position becomes rather embarrassing for Biblicists like myself to put forward. But I don't care whether it's popular or not, whether it's fashionable or not. This is what I believe that the Scripture is speaking about.

And I'll say one other thing before I get onto the next verse. These angels that sinned – and I think it's Jude or Peter. I always get those two muddled up – one of the two books in the New Testament – I think it's Jude says these angels are reserved in Hell. And that word is *Tarsus* for those of you that like to know these Greek words, and it simply means it's like a holding area, and they are awaiting their judgment. But like I say, these angels fell in the Old Testament, and by the time the New Covenant arrives and by the time men and women are born again, they become sons of God. And that doesn't mean that we are angelic, but we simply replace the fallen angels, and only when we get into adoption and glorification does that really make any sense to us.

VERSE 3: "And the LORD said, My spirit shall not always strive with man, for that he also is flesh: yet his days shall be an hundred and twenty years."

This also is referenced by those that believe that the sons of God are Adam's sons because the expression here is "man," and they don't believe that angels are spoken of as being men. Go to Mark, Mark 16 verse 5: "And entering into the sepulchre, they saw a young man sitting on the right side, clothed in a long white garment; and they were affrighted." Go to Matthew – Scripture with Scripture – Matthew 28 verse 5: **"And the angel answered and said unto the women, Fear not ye: for I know that ye seek Jesus, which was crucified."** So Scripture with Scripture we find that this man spoken of in Mark is an angel, according to Matthew's Gospel. So you can't use verse 3 from Genesis to shake off my position, my hypothesis that we are still looking at angels here, not necessarily men. The Bible is a bit deeper than people give it credit.

One other point to look at in verse 3 where it says that the Lord's Spirit won't strive with man for he is flesh and the days shall be 120 years, and I take that 120 years to be until the flood arrives, from this part of Scripture until the flood that Noah was told to prepare for. But this flesh – we'll get back to that in a minute that flesh and man are synonymous.

VERSE 4: "There were giants in the earth in those days; and also after that, when the sons of God came in unto the daughters of men, and they bare children to them, the same became mighty men which were of old, men of renown."

Three and four are certainly linked, and because these angels have taken on human form – and we're not told how they did it. Some have said it was through demon possession, which then allowed these angels to procreate, which they were never expected to do, they were never designed to do, and because they are going to create children with these women – and we're not told whether they were taken by force or whether it was wilful, and knowing how sinful people are and have been over history, I would say it was probably consensual. But the Lord is going to destroy all flesh because you've now got giants that have been born unto this unholy matrimony.

Just one other footnote to put forward before we go on. These giants which were born through this unholy union, no doubt one of these giants would be the ancestor to Goliath. And I remember watching that film "David and Bathsheba" starring Gregory Peck, and he's fighting Goliath in the film, and Goliath doesn't have six fingers. He has five fingers. Once again, Hollywood takes great liberties. And, yes, I know that Goliath's brother had six fingers – the Scripture makes that clear – but that's no reason to doubt that Goliath himself had anything less than six fingers. These are important omissions, and, once again, it proves that Hollywood is biased against the things of the Scripture, and we need to be better Bereans when it comes to these facts, these very important facts.

VERSE 5: "And GOD saw that the wickedness of man was great in the earth, and that every imagination of the thoughts of his heart was only evil continually."

Calvinists will use this part of Scripture to argue for total depravity, the first part of the TULIP, and most Calvinists would like to rename that to be total inability, which means that mankind, per se, is so wicked, he's so depraved that he can't tie his shoelaces unless the Lord allows him to do so. Now, I certainly believe that mankind pre-regeneration is in a state of wickedness, rebellion, so on and so forth, but I do not believe that you can show from the Scripture clearly and precisely this argument of total inability, this sort of zombie state which Calvinists would like you to believe. No doubt by verse 5 those that are on the earth are in great rebellion, but when we get to the next chapter, there's a man called Noah who got saved. So we can't say that everybody without exception is evil and wicked, but certainly Noah was the only one in his generation that got saved. But we cannot say, like I've already said, that everybody without exception was wicked and depraved – in the sense of total depravity, anyway.

VERSE 6: "And it repented the LORD that he had made man on the earth, and it grieved him at his heart."

This is such a sad, sad Scripture. The Lord is looking at His creation. Where are we? Chapter 6, Adam to Abraham is 2,000 years. We are just before Noah from chapter 7, so we are probably 5-, 600 years in, perhaps, and things are pretty bad. This expression "repent, repented," most of the new Bibles change that to "it regretted the Lord" or "it upset the Lord," but repented, repent normally means in this sense it regretted the Lord, but "repent" normally means a change of mind, a change of direction, and as we go through Genesis in other Scriptures, the word "repent" takes on a greater meaning.

VERSE 7: "And the LORD said, I will destroy man whom I have created from the face of the earth; both man, and beast, and the creeping thing, and the fowls of the air; for it repenteth me that I have made them."

No evolution there. This is creation, and I challenge Christians who don't believe in creation to repent and get back into creation. You need to defend the Scriptures; you need to defend creation. If we don't defend creation, if we don't stand up for creation, then where do you want to start? Which part of the Bible do you want to stand for? The first eleven chapters of Genesis are just as important as the following eleven chapters or the following eleven books. Every word of God is God-breathed. All Scripture is God-breathed. All Scripture is inspired of God. We cannot pick and choose which parts we like. Either God wrote everything through the Holy Spirit Who chose men to pen what He wanted them to pen, or He didn't do that. It's one or the other. We cannot pick and choose.

Beast, creeping thing, fowls of the air – everything is going to be destroyed by the time Noah gets to his flood. That, of course, needs to be clarified because Noah takes two of every kind onto the ark.

And, of course, the fishes and so on and so forth don't go onto the ark, which should be common sense; they stay in the water. But one of the reasons why these animals get destroyed – and you'll get animal lovers becoming rather upset when they hear these verses read out – is because man is so wicked, he's so depraved. Not only are women sleeping with demonic angels here from verses 2 and 3, but by verse 7, I believe this is a reference to bestiality, one of the most depraved acts ever, ever seen and witnessed in history when men and women have sex with animals – wicked. And, of course, it defiles the animals, and the Lord just destroys everyone and everything.

VERSE 8: "But Noah found grace in the eyes of the LORD."

What a remarkable Scripture. From 6, it said the Lord was grieved and it repented Him that He had made man, but by verse 8, Noah is certainly the exception here, and he has found grace in the eyes of the Lord. Some of our Calvinists, our friends, believe that faith in and of itself is a gift of God – and it's not. Paul mentions faith in 1 Corinthians, I think it's 1 Corinthians 12 as one of the gifts that are listed, but that sort of faith that Paul lists I've always believed it to be a reference to a missionary or somebody who's going to do something remarkable for the Lord. But grace itself, especially from Ephesians chapter 2, is the gift of God, and even John Calvin himself said that grace was the gift of God, not faith. Never mind this nonsense of decisional regeneration which is put forward by those that are Calvinists to those that aren't that somehow we have the power in and of ourselves to get saved when we make that decision. That is nonsense and it's a straw man. The only way that anybody ever got saved was by believing on the Lord Jesus Christ, and we got saved because Christ came to seek sinners. Again, this is very simple stuff, and I just wish people wouldn't get carried away with this intellectual approach – which is Calvinism – and get swept up in this. It's not necessary at all.

VERSE 9: "These are the generations of Noah: Noah was a just man and perfect in his generations, and Noah walked with God."

I love the last part of that, **"Noah walked with God."** Abraham is called a friend of God. The book of Hebrews says we are the brethren of the Lord Jesus Christ. It says here he was just and perfect. Of course, perfect here doesn't mean sinless. Only Jesus Christ was sinless. And when we get to, I think it's 7 or 8 of Genesis, Noah gets drunk, and it's the first reference to intoxication. And I will do a video on alcohol pretty soon. I've had different people ask me about what does the Bible say about alcohol. But like I say, Noah wasn't sinless, but in his own generation among his equals, if you will, among his generation, his colleagues – whatever expression you want to use – he was perfect in that period of time.

VERSES 10-11: "And Noah begat three sons, Shem, Ham, and Japheth. The earth also was corrupt before God, and the earth was filled with violence."

Nothing much changes.

VERSES 12-13: "And God looked upon the earth, and, behold, it was corrupt; for all flesh had corrupted his way upon the earth. And God said unto Noah, The end of all flesh is come before me; for the earth is filled with violence through them; and, behold, I will destroy them with the earth."

Just keep this in mind that this solar system was created by the triune God, and the triune God has the rights, He has the deeds to the solar system. Everything that we can see and hear and read about has the Lord's fingerprints on it, and because that is the case, the Lord is more than eligible, He's more than justified to do whatever He chooses to do. If He wanted to, He could wipe out everything tomorrow, but He hasn't chosen to do that. It's like the people who say, "Why does the Lord allow so much evil in the world? Why does He allow all this wickedness? Why doesn't He destroy it all?" Well, if He did, we would all be destroyed, period. Most people that get saved have a lot of baggage, and if they're honest with themselves, they would have been destroyed many years ago if the Lord hadn't been longsuffering, not willing that any would perish. And they got saved through the Lord's longsuffering.

But, like I say, the Lord would have every right to just click His fingers and everything would be consigned to everlasting Hell, but that's not what He's chosen to do. And He was quite at liberty to use Israel throughout the Old Testament as a sort of type of police force, a type of army to destroy wickedness and sin on the earth. And if you are a non-Christian and you believe in evolution, then it's very difficult for you to condemn that, because you have no absolutes; you believe it's survival of the fittest, and because you would have us believe that we came from animals, then it's very hard for you to look back, especially over the last 100 years or so, and criticise anything that came out of Nazi Germany or Communist Russia – again, survival of the fittest. But the Lord is merciful, and He found a way to be reconciled to sinful man.

Okay. 14, 15 and 16, Noah is given clear instructions as to how to build this ark, and 16 says only one window was to be built into this ark, and the second part of 16 says it's going to be three stories. And the measurements are given as being 300 cubits, and that's probably in length, and 50 cubits wide and 30 cubits high. Now, I think in modern English, that's about 450 feet long. And Patrick wrote an article on Noah's ark some years ago, and I think when he first wrote the article, we looked at the measurements then, and 300 cubits translates to about 450 feet long, if my memory serves me right; and 450 feet long is the equivalent to the British aircraft carriers HMS Invincible, Illustrious, and Ark Royal, and they are 450 feet in length and they are about –

I think it's 20- to 40,000 tons. And we went on Illustrious last year, which, again, is the same as Ark Royal and Invincible, and if my measurements are right, then Noah's ark is going to be the same length as the British aircraft carriers, which are pretty big. They're not as big as the American carriers, but they're pretty big nonetheless. And it says it's going to be three flights and, like I say, 30 cubits high. So it's pretty big.

And a lot of people, especially dispensationalists, believe that Noah was pretty big, and when I say "big," I mean quite tall. And some have argued that Adam was a sort of giant in and of himself and Noah has retained that height. Now, again, we can't prove that from Scripture so I'm not even going to go there or even allude to that. But this is a pretty big ark, and he's got help from his sons, of course.

VERSE 17: "And, behold, I, even I, do bring a flood of waters upon the earth, to destroy all flesh, wherein is the breath of life, from under heaven; and every thing that is in the earth shall die."

Again, this is the Lord's universe. He is the landlord of this earth, and when He says time's up, time's up.

VERSE 18. "But with thee will I establish my covenant; and thou shalt come into the ark, thou, and thy sons, and thy wife, and thy sons' wives with thee."

This covenant was a one-off covenant never repeated again. And I want to say also that Noah wasn't saved by building an ark. There are no works involved here. Noah was saved by his faith in the Lord, and that faith produced works which built an ark. And I've said this in other videos that we don't want to get into this sort of two-tier system of salvation that church-age saints are saved by grace through faith alone, which they certainly are, and yet Old Testament saints like Noah, for example, and Tribulation saints are saved by faith and works and therefore in eternity you're going to have people like Noah and Tribulation saints boasting that they did it their way, like the old Paul Anka song goes, but church-age saints got there through faith in Christ alone. It cannot be acceptable to teach such a thing. Like I say, Noah had faith. That saved him, and he built an ark, and that was a covenant which started with Noah and ended with Noah.

VERSE 19: "And of every living thing of all flesh, two of every sort shalt thou bring into the ark, to keep them alive with thee; they shall be male and female."

That should be obvious as to why.

VERSES 20-22: "Of fowls after their kind, and of cattle after their kind, of every creeping thing of the earth after his kind, two of every sort shall come unto thee, to keep them alive. And take thou unto thee of all food that is eaten, and thou shalt gather it to thee; and it shall be for food for thee, and for them. Thus did Noah; according to all that God commanded him, so did he."

And, of course, that concludes the sixth chapter of Genesis.

Just one final thing to share with you before we get to the seventh chapter. There was a film made back in the sixties by John Houston, and he plays Noah, and it's actually quite a good film. I haven't watched it in several years. It's one of the better films that have been made by Hollywood concerning the Bible. And that won't surprise you, of course, that most of their films are pretty poor for obvious reasons. But this is one of the better films, and I think in the film, if my memory serves me right, that he actually talks to the animals and he sort of ushers them into the ark. And it's possible that that may have happened. Adam named the animals back in the Garden, and Eve is talking to the serpent and he's talking back to her. So there was certainly something quite remarkable during this early period of the

Scriptures. And, of course, during the thousand-year reign, it will be repeated again – humans lying down with animals and having world peace. But until then, there will be wars and rumours of wars.

Just before I get into Genesis chapter 7, I want to say that Patrick has written an article about the flood of Noah, and what I'm going to do is link his article in the description box if you're watching this video on YouTube, and if you're not watching it on YouTube, you can go onto our website and look in the general articles of interest, and I think it's called "The Great Ark of Noah." And he goes through the flood and lists some pretty interesting information, which I think will supplement this video quite nicely. But I won't be going through every verse in this chapter. I'm going to pick out just a few verses and, as always, offer my thoughts as I go through this bit of Scripture.

CHAPTER 7

VERSE 1: "And the LORD said unto Noah, Come thou and all thy house into the ark; for thee have I seen righteous before me in this generation."

Noah was the only man that got saved during his time; and, of course, his sons and his wife and their wives joined Noah. They went on the ark with him – a bit like Lot. Lot got saved before he fell into decline, and he managed to get his daughters to leave Sodom and Gomorrah, and his wife went with him, but, of course, her heart wasn't with the Lord - it was with her husband - and, of course, she looked back and the Lord consumed her. But here Noah is saved and his faith carries his family with him. And somebody once said that the Lord is in the business of not only getting one person in a family saved, but He's in the business of getting an entire family saved; and for some of us, that hasn't yet come to pass, but I know that for a few of you watching this video, that has been the case in your own lives.

Just one more comment to make on this expression **"house."** If you go to Matthew chapter 7, I want to show you two references in the New Testament that talk about a house in a sort of corporate manner. Look at verse 24, Matthew 7:24: **"Therefore whosoever heareth these sayings of mine, and doeth them, I will liken him unto a wise man, which built his house upon a rock: And the rain descended, and the floods came, and the winds blew, and beat upon that house; and it fell not: for it was founded upon a rock. And every one that heareth these sayings of mine, and doeth them not, shall be likened unto a foolish man, which built his house upon the sand: And the rain descended, and the floods came, and the winds blew, and beat upon that house; and it fell: and great was the fall of it"** (vv. 24-27.)

Now, you've got two things going on here. You've got a literal house being spoken about built on sand, and that is obviously a recipe for disaster. But you've also got a spiritual application here. Go to Hebrews chapter 3 verse 5: **"And Moses verily was faithful in all his house, as a servant, for a testimony of those things which were to be spoken after; But Christ as a son over his own house; whose house are we, if we hold fast the confidence and the rejoicing of the hope firm unto the end"** (vv. 5-6.)

So this expression **"house"** ultimately in the New Covenant means to be in the body of Christ, and therefore you belong to the Lord Jesus Christ. And, of course, Acts 16 says if you believe on the Lord Jesus Christ, you and your house will be saved. And you need to keep in mind that those in the house of the Philippian jailer also believed in the Lord and got saved. You don't get the head of the family getting saved and by default everybody else gets saved. That's not what is meant by that expression.

This reference to the ark is going to have some imagery, I put to you, in the Tribulation. Once the Rapture has occurred, there will be people still on the earth that are going to get saved, and they're going to go through the Tribulation and survive, and Matthew 24 says that the angels gather together those that are left on the earth and take them to be with the Lord. And some of our post-tribulational brethren believe that is a reference to a rapture, a *harpazo* or a catching away or somebody said "the great snatch." Now, I don't believe that it is. How the saints are going to be taken to Jerusalem is irrelevant in many ways, but like I say, this ark that Noah and his family entered into preserves them, and that's a type of a New Testament saint.

VERSE 4: "For yet seven days, and I will cause it to rain upon the earth forty days and forty nights; and every living substance that I have made will I destroy from off the face of the earth."

The Lord owns the earth. He owns everything that He has created, and like a painter, if He wants to destroy His painting, He can and nobody has any right to question it. When judgment comes, it certainly comes, and everything and everyone that wasn't marked out to be preserved is destroyed. Of course, the ark is going to be big enough to take quite a lot of animals to be used after the flood to once again replenish the earth.

VERSE 5: "And Noah did according unto all that the LORD commanded him."

Faith without works is dead, says the book of James, and I have no problem turning that around and saying works without faith is dead also. We have a lot of celebrities raising money during periods of crisis, catastrophes. There's a famine here, there's an earthquake there, there's a flood here, there's a volcano there – whatever it is – and all of the celebrities, the multimillionaires will get together and try and raise lots of money. And if you watch this very carefully, you will see that they don't normally give any of their own money. They'll go on sponsored walks; they'll go on sponsored swims; they'll do these telethons. I think it was Jerry Lewis in America for many, many years had an annual telethon, and all of the greats would go on this telethon, and they'd be on the phones hours on end trying to raise money. And I've often thought, if all these celebrities sat down and just wrote out a check for half a million pounds each or a million dollars each – whatever currency is relevant to your country – if all these celebrities got together and just wrote out a check, they could alleviate a lot of problems in the world overnight. But what they don't like doing a lot of the time is spending their own money. They're quite happy for you to spend your money, but they won't spend their money.

VERSES 6-7: "And Noah was six hundred years old when the flood of waters was upon the earth. And Noah went in, and his sons, and

his wife, and his sons' wives with him, into the ark, because of the waters of the flood."

These daughters of Noah's sons are probably espoused to his sons, and, of course, in ancient times, in times of antiquity and especially in the history of the Jews, once you were engaged to your husband-to-be or your wife-to-be, that was a legally binding contract and you were now considered man and wife. Even though you hadn't been officially married, you hadn't consummated marriage, you were still legally married in the eyes of the Lord. And ultimately when flesh meets flesh, that also constitutes a marriage. But from a legal standpoint, once an engagement has been announced, then the couple is legally married in the eyes of the Lord.

VERSES 9-12: "There went in two and two unto Noah into the ark, the male and the female, as God had commanded Noah. And it came to pass after seven days, that the waters of the flood were upon the earth. In the six hundredth year of Noah's life, in the second month, the seventeenth day of the month, the same day were all the fountains of the great deep broken up, and the windows of heaven were opened. And the rain was upon the earth forty days and forty nights."

Now, again, I'm not going to go through every verse here and offer my thoughts. Read the article which is in the description box and you can cross reference that with the Scripture, which you should always do anyway. But this, I believe, is a worldwide flood. I've always believed that, and I have no reason to doubt it. And as you can see, Noah is – what? – 600 years old, and he's built an ark from scratch. And like I've said in the previous clip, Noah wasn't saved by building an ark, as impressive as it was. And even to this day we believe it has been moored on Mount Ararat, which is on the Turkish border, and there have been a lot of people from the 18th century right up to recent years that claim to have seen it. Some have claimed to have even taken wood cuttings from it. But there have been images from, I think, American spy planes back in the 50s, and they've taken snaps of it. So there is something there and like I said in the last clip, 450 feet long is the measurements of the ark, which is the equivalent to the UK aircraft carriers. And they are currently building two new carriers which will be a lot bigger than the current carriers. But, like I say, it has been found, but it's on a very sensitive border. And, of course, Turkey is in Islamic country, so they wouldn't be in any rush to affirm something from the book of Genesis.

VERSES 13-15: "In the selfsame day entered Noah, and Shem, and Ham, and Japheth, the sons of Noah, and Noah's wife, and the three wives of his sons with them, into the ark; They, and every beast after his kind, and all the cattle after their kind, and every creeping thing that creepeth upon the earth after his kind, and every fowl after his kind, every bird of every sort. And they went in unto Noah into the ark, two and two of all flesh, wherein is the breath of life."

There's not much to add to these verses. It's quite obvious that the Lord wants these animals to survive the flood, and as I said in the previous clip, the fishes, all of the sea creatures that the Lord had made are going to be preserved in the flood. They don't need to go onto the ark. But these creeping things, these cattle and every other beast after his kind are going to be preserved. Look at 16: **"And they that went in, went in male and female of all flesh, as God had commanded him: and the LORD shut him in."**

Now, I believe in eternal security. I believe that my salvation doesn't depend on me gripping the Lord's hand tight every moment of every day. I don't believe in getting on my knees every night and confessing all of my sins to stay saved. I believe that when I believed on the Lord, He saved me and He keeps me saved.

And I want to say something else. In fact, I want to show you a Scripture, and I'm going to give you an analogy here. Go to Ephesians chapter 4 verse 30: "And grieve not the holy Spirit of God, whereby ye are sealed unto the day of redemption." And I'll show you one more from the first chapter, Ephesians 1:13: **"In whom ye also trusted, after that ye heard the word of truth, the gospel of your salvation: in whom also after that ye believed, ye were sealed with that holy Spirit of promise."** I believe in the preservation of the saints. I believe that when a man or woman gets saved, it's up to the Lord to keep that person saved and bring him spotless or bring her spotless unto the Lord.

Picture yourself on an airplane, shall we say, and you're flying from A to B, and you get on the plane, you sort your baggage out, you sit down, and you've got a, let's say, a six-hour flight or seven-hour flight ahead of you. It doesn't depend on you to get the crew from A to B. It doesn't depend on you to ensure that flight has a safe journey. You can run up and down the plane. You can be sick in the toilet. You can do all the things that people do when they travel. You can close your eyes. You can lose yourself for those hours on a plane. But going from A to B safely doesn't depend on you. That's a job of the captain. And Jesus is the Captain of our souls. He's the Captain of our salvation. We sit in the plane and we trust the captain to get us from A to B. Of course, you can be apprehensive; you can be a good passenger or you can be a bad passenger and do stupid things on the plane, but it's not down to you to land that plane. That's down to the captain.

And when it says here that **"the Lord shut him in,"** I would say it was impossible, totally impossible for Noah to get himself out of the ark. That's my position. Now, there are a lot of people that hold to conditional security, and I'm afraid to say that most people, most Christians that I know – in fact, I'll go even further than that and say the overwhelming majority of Christians that I know hold to conditional security; and that, in reality, is Roman Catholicism because these people, as good as they are in many ways – and I know most of them personally and I know most of them are saved. I don't doubt their salvation, but in essence they are practicing a Catholic doctrine, a doctrine that means in essence that they have to confess their sins every day because they might lose their salvation. And I've asked people in the past to give me an answer to a question which was along these lines: That if you were saved at midday and at 10 past 12 you got into a blazing row with your husband or your wife and you physically assaulted that person, and you got into your car and you drove down the road and got into a car crash and you died, would you go to Heaven or Hell? And nearly everybody that I've asked says they'd go to Hell because they hadn't repented. That, of course, is not justification; that's not Sola Fide. That is infused righteousness, not imputed righteousness. And I've already talked about that in other videos, so if you want to go into it a bit deeper, just Google it.

VERSE 17: "And the flood was forty days upon the earth; and the waters increased, and bare up the ark, and it was lift up above the earth."

This doesn't mean that the ark went into space, which some people might think it means. It simply means that it was lifted up into the air. And if you go to 2 Samuel 18:9, it speaks about Absalom being caught in a tree, and it says **"he was taken up between the heaven and the earth; and the mule that was under him went away"** – a sort of reference to hanging. He's caught in a tree, and his feet are dangling from the earth, but, of course, he's not in heaven, per se, and he's not on the earth. His feet are off the ground. It's simply a sort of bit of poetic language, if you will.

VERSES 18-19: "And the waters prevailed, and were increased greatly upon the earth; and the ark went upon the face of the waters.

And the waters prevailed exceedingly upon the earth; and all the high hills, that were under the whole heaven, were covered."

Again, nothing survives this flood. Everything and everyone is going to be completely destroyed.

VERSE 20: "Fifteen cubits upward did the waters prevail; and the mountains were covered."

Every mountain, every hill on planet earth was covered, and we know that Mount Ararat was 17,000 feet high, and that got covered by over 22 miles. So this is a massive worldwide flood.

VERSE 21: "And all flesh died that moved upon the earth, both of fowl, and of cattle, and of beast, and of every creeping thing that creepeth upon the earth, and every man:"

I just want to add a quick footnote to verse 21. The previous video, we looked at the sons of God committing fornication with the daughters of men, and they produced this offspring, this sort of cross-human, cross-demonic offspring which resulted in giants walking on the earth. And it must have been so serious that the Lord simply destroyed everything. When He gets to Sodom and Gomorrah, He doesn't destroy the entire world; He just destroys the areas around Sodom and Gomorrah. And, of course, Lot's daughters think that they are the only people left on the earth, and they do an Adam and Eve and they re-populate the earth.

But these demons, these devils that were involved in chapter 6 I've spoken of in 2 Peter 2:4: **"For if God spared not the angels that sinned, but cast them down to hell, and delivered them into chains of darkness, to be reserved unto judgment; And spared not the old world, but saved Noah the eighth person, a preacher of righteousness, bringing in the flood upon the world of the ungodly"** (vv. 4-5.) And, of course, Jude 6 and 7 also speaks about this.

What we can't say for sure is if other angels fell after these angels were put into Hell, into this holding area and did something similar later on which produced the line of Goliath. We can't rule that out completely. Either way, it was so serious, as I say, that the Lord just destroyed everybody and everything and chose Himself just Noah's little family. So just a theory that I have that somehow Genesis 6 is going to feed into Goliath's line. Of course, David destroys Goliath, and David is a type of Christ, and the Gospel of Luke says as it was in the days of Noah, so shall it be in the days of the Son of man (Lk. 17:26.) So there is a link between Genesis 6 and the Second Advent. We're not sure exactly what it's going to entail, but you don't need to read too far between the lines to work out what is being referenced there.

VERSE 22: "All in whose nostrils was the breath of life, of all that was in the dry land, died."

Again, quite clear. Nothing as of this day has survived.

VERSES 23-24: "And every living substance was destroyed which was upon the face of the ground, both man, and cattle, and the creeping things, and the fowl of the heaven; and they were destroyed from the earth: and Noah only remained alive, and they that were with him in the ark. And the waters prevailed upon the earth an hundred and fifty days."

So, like I say, Noah is the only person that is saved, that has been saved throughout this period and those that were on the ark. And that is the condition – that you get into the ark and you stay in the ark. And as I've already said from verse 16, the Lord shut him in, and only the Lord can let you out. And I do not believe in conditional security. I believe that once a person has been truly saved, truly born again – not this one, two, three, pray with me stuff, but truly born again, truly regenerated, then it's the Lord's job to get you from A to B. And you can be as good as you want to be, and you won't stay saved, and you can be as bad as you want to be, and you won't lose your salvation. Your salvation doesn't depend on you; it depends on the work of the Lord Jesus Christ.

Twenty-four: **"And the waters prevailed upon the earth an hundred and fifty days."** It's quite obvious that this flood isn't going to be over in five minutes; it's going to last 150 days.

CHAPTER 8

Okay. This video will be a continuation from my series back in the summer, which started going through the book of Genesis, and I managed to record the first seven chapters, but due to other projects and commitments, I had to put this rather mammoth task on hold and come back to it. But, Lord willing, I want to continue on now, and today I want to look at chapter 8 verse 1.

VERSES 1-3: "And God remembered Noah, and every living thing, and all the cattle that was with him in the ark: and God made a wind to pass over the earth, and the waters asswaged; The fountains also of the deep and the windows of heaven were stopped, and the rain from heaven was restrained; And the waters returned from off the earth continually: and after the end of the hundred and fifty days the waters were abated."

Several points I want to flag up. First of all, verse 1 says, **"God remembered Noah."** In the sixth chapter, eighth verse it says, **"Noah found grace in the eyes of the LORD."** The only way that anyone is ever going to be saved is by their faith in the Lord.

Go to the book of Hebrews. I've just finished going through Hebrews, thirteen chapters, and in total it came to three and a half hours. And if you want to listen to that, you can do so. But Hebrews 13 verse 5: **"Let your conversation be without covetousness; and be content with such things as ye have:"** – now, watch this – **"for he hath said, I will never leave thee, nor forsake thee."** Okay. So if you're one of His, you will always be one of His – once saved, always saved. Go to the book of Matthew, Matthew chapter 7, speaking about the Kingdom of Heaven, which has two parts – it has a physical realm and a spiritual realm, and

I'll come back to that in a minute. Look at verse 21, Matthew 7:21: **"Not every one that saith unto me, Lord, Lord, shall enter into the kingdom of heaven; but he that doeth the will of my Father which is in heaven."** And the Gospel of John chapter 6 tells you that the will of the Father was to believe on the Son of God. Twenty-two: **"Many"** – not just some – **"Many will say to me in that day, Lord, Lord, have we not prophesied in thy name? and in thy name have cast out devils? and in thy name done many wonderful works? And then will I profess unto them, I never knew you: depart from me, ye that work iniquity"** (vv. 22-23.) If you were saved for ten, fifteen, twenty years or so and then fell into sin and never dealt with it, then you would die and go straight to Heaven. Why? Well, Jesus Christ cannot deny Himself. He cannot say that He never knew you even though you fell into sin. Go to 2 Timothy – don't worry, I'll get back to Genesis in a minute – 2 Timothy chapter 2 verse 11: **"It is a faithful saying: For if we be dead with him"** – there's our spiritual rebirth – **"we shall also live with him: If we suffer, we shall also reign with him: if we deny him, he also will deny us"** (vv. 11-12.) Again, that's a reference to the Millennium, not your salvation. Thirteen: **"If we believe not, yet he abideth faithful: he cannot deny himself."** If you're saved, you are saved.

Matthew 7 – just a quick footnote here – is talking about the Kingdom of Heaven, and I do believe that the Kingdom of Heaven and the Kingdom of God are the same thing; however, there are two applications to this. The Kingdom of Heaven, first and foremost, can be a spiritual or a physical place, if you will. The spiritual realm would be here and now. Paul speaks about the Kingdom of God in Romans 13, I think it is, and Acts 28, whereas the Kingdom of Heaven can also be a physical realm, a literal realm. Matthew 25 would be a good cross reference for this when Christ comes back at the end of the Tribulation; and all the nations are standing before Him, and He judges the nations, and then the thousand year reign commences.

So just a quick recap. The Kingdom of Heaven and the Kingdom of God are the same thing but they have two applications – physical realm and a spiritual realm. And here this is speaking about "in that day," and in that day could either be the beginning of the Great White Throne where the whole world will stand before Christ, all those that are not saved – the saved man and woman won't be standing there, but all of the unsaved people will stand there – or it could have a reference to the commencement of the thousand year reign. But maybe on another video I will go a little deeper into this.

Go back to Genesis. That was just a quick detour. God remembered Noah and every living thing, and God made a wind to pass over the earth and the waters asswaged. The Lord Himself brought the flood on the world as punishment for sin. God is holy, God is righteous, and He won't tolerate sin. And if you look at the seventh chapter, verse 16, it says, **"and the LORD shut him in."** Noah's job was to build the ark, and once the ark was built, he got into it with his wife, his sons, and his daughters-in-law, and the rest was over to the Lord. There was no rudder on this boat, on this ship, if you will. The Lord was the Captain.

But just picture this if you will. Here you find Noah in a sense like a captain, if you will, a captain of his ship. Go to Matthew's Gospel, back to Matthew, Matthew chapter 8. I want to try and show you a slight parallel here. Matthew 8 verse 19: **"And a certain scribe came, and said unto him, Master, I will follow thee whithersoever thou goest"** – similar sort of language. Noah was told to build an ark, get into it, and sit tight. Look at 20: **"And Jesus saith unto him, The foxes have holes, and the birds of the air have nests; but the Son of man hath not where to lay his head"** – no castles, no palaces. He had nowhere to lay His head. Twenty-one: **"And another of his disciples said unto him, Lord, suffer me first to go and bury my father. But Jesus said unto him, Follow me; and let the dead bury their dead"** (vv. 21-22.) – pretty clear language: Follow Me and I will give you rest. The last part of John's Gospel Jesus says, **"Follow thou me."** We follow the Lord Jesus Christ. We don't follow popes, cardinals, prophets, apostles, soothsayers, clairvoyance – whatever group of people you would care to name. We follow the Lord Jesus Christ, and the word of God is our final written authority.

Verse 23: **"And when he was entered into a ship, his disciples followed him."** Hebrews says that Christ is the Captain of our salvation, and here He's going to enter into a ship. Twenty-four: **"And, behold, there arose a great tempest in the sea, insomuch that the ship was covered with the waves: but he was asleep."** Look at 26: **"And he saith unto them, Why are ye fearful, O ye of little faith? Then he arose, and rebuked the winds and the sea; and there was a great calm. But the men marvelled, saying, What manner of man is this, that even the winds and the sea obey him!"** (vv. 26-27.) So there you find the Lord Jesus Christ having control over the elements, over nature, and only the Lord God could do so. Satan is a created being. He has a very limited mandate, and post the death of the Lord Jesus Christ, he's even more diminished, although he does go around like a roaring lion seeking to devour whom he will. Nonetheless, his power is certainly limited, and all these groups, all these Satanists that call themselves the church of Satan that follow this fallen angel would do well to read the book of Revelation, because he will go into the lake of fire. And if you're following him, then you are going to go down a cul-de-sac.

So just a quick parallel between the great flood and the temporary storm on the lake of Galilee. And I've been there. It's a very peaceful part of Israel. And in Genesis 8 and Matthew 8 the Lord Himself intervened and dealt with the storm.

VERSE 4: "And the ark rested in the seventh month, on the seventeenth day of the month, upon the mountains of Ararat."

There's your modern-day Turkey.

VERSES 5-11: "And the waters decreased continually until the tenth month: in the tenth month, on the first day of the month, were the tops of the mountains seen. And it came to pass at the end of forty days, that Noah opened the window of the ark which he had made: And he sent forth a raven, which went forth to and fro, until the waters were dried up from off the earth. Also he sent forth a dove from him, to see if the waters were abated from off the face of the ground; But the dove found no rest for the sole of her foot" – interesting she's spoken of in the feminine – **"and she returned unto him into the ark, for the waters were on the face of the whole earth"** – this is not a local flood; this is a global flood – **"then he put forth his hand, and took her, and pulled her in unto him into the ark. And he stayed yet other seven days; and again he sent forth the dove out of the ark; And the dove came in to him in the evening; and, lo, in her mouth was an olive leaf pluckt off: so Noah knew that the waters were abated from off the earth."**

Romans 11 speaks about the church being grafted in and the root remaining holy. John 15, Jesus speaks about the vine and how we are to abide in Him; otherwise, the branch will be broken off. And, of course, the olive leaf and the trees are used in the Gospels and in Judges to refer to the nation of Israel.

VERSES 12-14: "And he stayed yet other seven days; and sent forth the dove; which returned not again unto him any more. And it came to pass in the six hundredth and first year, in the first month, the first day of the month, the waters were dried up from off the earth: and Noah removed the covering of the ark, and looked, and, behold, the face of the ground was dry. And in the second month, on the seven and twentieth day of the month, was the earth dried."

Noah has been in the ark for over a year, and, like I say, he was told to build the ark, get into the ark, and Jesus as the Captain of our salvation got Noah from A to B. And that's pretty much how our salvation works. We believe on Him, we trust Him, and then we live by faith.

VERSES 15-19: "And God spake unto Noah, saying, Go forth of the ark, thou, and thy wife, and thy sons, and thy sons' wives with thee. Bring forth with thee every living thing that is with thee, of all flesh, both of fowl, and of cattle, and of every creeping thing that creepeth upon the earth; that they may breed abundantly in the earth, and be fruitful, and multiply upon the earth. And Noah went forth, and his sons, and his wife, and his sons' wives with him: Every beast, every creeping thing, and every fowl, and whatsoever creepeth upon the earth, after their kinds, went forth out of the ark."

Nineteen makes it quite clear that the Lord not only preserved Noah and his family but all of the animals that went onto the ark too – much like an airplane. You get onto a plane, and you trust the pilot to get you from A to B. That is a similar picture to how our salvation works. We believe on the Lord; we trust Him, and Scripture says that He will bring to pass the work which He has commenced, which He has begun.

VERSES 20-22: "And Noah builded an altar unto the LORD; and took of every clean beast, and of every clean fowl, and offered burnt offerings on the altar. And the LORD smelled a sweet savour; and the LORD said in his heart, I will not again curse the ground any more for man's sake; for the imagination of man's heart is evil from his youth; neither will I again smite any more every thing living, as I have done. While the earth remaineth, seedtime and harvest, and cold and heat, and summer and winter, and day and night shall not cease."

CHAPTER 9

VERSE 1: "And God blessed Noah and his sons, and said unto them, Be fruitful, and multiply, and replenish the earth."

Adam and Eve were told to replenish the earth, and Noah's sons were also told to do the same. And when we get to the later part of Genesis, you'll find that Lot's daughters took upon themselves to do the same thing. They were of the impression that nobody was on the earth. They thought that the earth had been destroyed; hence, they got their father drunk and committed a sexual act with him. And I will try and tie that in with the later part of the ninth chapter.

VERSE 2: "And the fear of you and the dread of you shall be upon every beast of the earth, and upon every fowl of the air, upon all that moveth upon the earth, and upon all the fishes of the sea; into your hand are they delivered."

The Lord has given man dominion over the earth. Man was made in the image of God, not animal. And that doesn't allow man to treat animal as he chooses to. It's always despicable when we see rare animals, almost extinct animals being hunted just for the fun of it. But here it says the fear and the dread of you shall be upon every beast of the earth. And don't forget, back in the Garden, Adam named the animals, and there's every reason to believe that Adam was able to speak to the animals, and they spoke to him too.

VERSES 3-4: "Every moving thing that liveth shall be meat for you; even as the green herb have I given you all things. But flesh with the life thereof, which is the blood thereof, shall ye not eat."

Pre fall man was a vegetarian. Post fall, man was able to eat animals, and, of course, animals eat animals. But in the Millennium, you're going to have a throwback to the Garden of Eden.

VERSES 5-6: "And surely your blood of your lives will I require; at the hand of every beast will I require it, and at the hand of man; at the hand of every man's brother will I require the life of man. Whoso sheddeth man's blood, by man shall his blood be shed: for in the image of God made he man."

Quite simple. If a person takes another person's life, that is considered murder, and the guilty party would be put to death. Now, this throws out a lot of other issues – just wars. Do nations have the right to invade and then launch a war and kill people along the way? Well, there's a difference between killing and murdering, and, yes, we know the Hebrew says "murder" not "kill," but nonetheless there is a clear distinction between the state killing an enemy and an individual within that state murdering somebody else.

VERSE 7: "And you, be ye fruitful, and multiply; bring forth abundantly in the earth, and multiply therein."

Just one other quick point which I don't want to miss out. It says, "for in the image of God made He man." Everybody living on the earth today is made in the image of God. Okay. There are some people which believe that we're made in the image of Adam, but, then, Adam is made in the image of God. So you can't really get around it. Paul also speaks about man being made in the image of God, and here the reason why the Lord is not content to let a man kill another man for no good reason is because for that very purpose – he's made in God's image. He reflects the Lord's hunger for justice, to some extent, the Lord's goodness, the Lord's mercy. Even though man is flawed, even though man is depraved, he still has the image of God imprinted in his DNA.

VERSES 8-11: "And God spake unto Noah, and to his sons with him, saying, And I, behold, I establish my covenant with you, and with your seed after you; And with every living creature that is with you, of the fowl, of the cattle, and of every beast of the earth with you; from all that go out of the ark, to every beast of the earth. And I will establish my covenant with you; neither shall all flesh be cut off any more by the waters of a flood; neither shall there any more be a flood to destroy the earth."

Second Peter speaks of a great fire and the elements burning, and the Lord is going to pretty much break up the earth as we know it today, and that will happen during the Tribulation, and then we'll get a new heaven and the new earth. But there will be no more floods.

VERSE 12: "And God said, This is the token of the covenant which I make between me and you and every living creature that is with you, for perpetual generations:"

If that word **"perpetual"** was on its own, it would simply mean eternal, but when you put **"generations"** after it, it has a more limited connotation to it.

VERSE 13: "I do set my bow in the cloud, and it shall be for a token of a covenant between me and the earth."

Bow means rainbow.

VERSES 14-15: "And it shall come to pass, when I bring a cloud over the earth, that the bow shall be seen in the cloud: And I will remember my covenant, which is between me and you and every living creature of all flesh; and the waters shall no more become a flood to destroy all flesh."

This is an unconditional covenant. Noah had no say whatsoever in this - similar to the covenant which He made with Abraham, which we will get to later on. But this is a covenant first and foremost given to Noah.

VERSE 16: "And the bow shall be in the cloud; and I will look upon it, that I may remember the everlasting covenant between God and every living creature of all flesh that is upon the earth."

Pretty clear English – everlasting. Nothing about generations there, so you can go from the time of Noah right up until the Millennium.

VERSES 17-18: "And God said unto Noah, This is the token of the covenant, which I have established between me and all flesh that is upon the earth. And the sons of Noah, that went forth of the ark, were Shem, and Ham, and Japheth: and Ham is the father of Canaan."

Cain, of course, is the first murderer in the Bible, and he's got a pretty bad line. The Antichrist, some people believe, also comes from the line of Cain.

VERSE 19: "These are the three sons of Noah: and of them was the whole earth overspread."

Pretty amazing that three men created 5 1/2 billion people many thousands of years later.

VERSES 20-21: "And Noah began to be an husbandman, and he planted a vineyard: And he drank of the wine, and was drunken; and he was uncovered within his tent."

This is a pretty sad part of Scripture. It's not clear whether this was the first time this ever happened or not. It's not clear whether Noah intentionally got drunk or not. I'm prepared to give Noah the benefit of the doubt. I suggest this was a first-time event, and because he fell, you're going to see what happens when a godly man falls.

VERSES 22-23: "And Ham, the father of Canaan, saw the nakedness of his father, and told his two brethren without" – old English for outside – **"And Shem and Japheth took a garment, and laid it upon both their shoulders, and went backward, and covered the nakedness of their father; and their faces were backward, and they saw not their father's nakedness."**

When a righteous man falls, two things will happen: First of all, those that are saved, those that love the Lord, those that are walking with the Lord will never rejoice in this. Those that are unsaved and those that are carnal will make quite a noise about that. And what you're looking at, really, are enemies of God. This was a good man, Noah, and his son was a bad man. And I think his son took great delight to see his father fall – very, very tragic.

VERSES 24-25: "And Noah awoke from his wine, and knew what his younger son had done unto him. And he said, Cursed be Canaan; a servant of servants shall he be unto his brethren."

Nothing in the Scripture to suggest any sexual act on Ham's part. Nonetheless, he's woken up, and probably his other two sons have told him that Ham was out to embarrass him, to humiliate him. And his anger is pretty righteous; he's pretty justified; he's going to curse Ham. Some people take this part of Scripture to suggest that this is where the black people come into play, but I'm not convinced of that. I think at the Tower of Babel the Lord struck all the races, and that's where your Asians, that's where your Orientals, and that's where your Negros come into play. But here he's cursed; he's put down. Look at 26: **"And he said, Blessed be the LORD God of Shem; and Canaan shall be his servant."**

That's pretty much his curse, really. He's going to now serve his older brother, which he would have done anyway because obviously Shem was the oldest.

VERSE 27: "God shall enlarge Japheth" – the youngest – **"and he shall dwell in the tents of Shem; and Canaan shall be his servant."**

He's now going to serve his older and his younger brother – Pretty humiliating.

VERSES 28-29: "And Noah lived after the flood three hundred and fifty years. And all the days of Noah were nine hundred and fifty years: and he died."

Noah is a type of Christ, as I say in the eighth chapter. He built an ark and he got his family onto the ark and the animals, and the Lord preserved them and brought them out at the other end. There is application to suggest that Noah is a type of Jew in the Tribulation that will go through and come out at the other end, whereas we are looking at the church, those that are living today to be raptured before the Tribulation, and we look at people like Enoch who was simply raptured, simply taken out, and he's a good picture of the church; he's a type of the church.

But like I said at the start of this video, Lot's daughters fell into a period of anguish. They didn't know exactly what had happened. The earth, they thought, had been destroyed, and they would have gone back to the account of the Noah flood, and they took it upon themselves to re-populate the earth. Lot was a good man. That's why they got him drunk. If he hadn't been a good man, he wouldn't have had to get drunk. And Noah was a good man but on this occasion got drunk, and his son, his middle son made a mockery of his father.

And I'll just say one final point. Alcohol in the Scripture is never spoken of in a godly way. Paul refers to alcohol as a form of medication in 1 Timothy. Proverbs speaks about medicine and alcohol being used interchangeably. But apart from medicine, apart from alleviating pain, alcohol is never spoken of in a positive sense. And one of the biggest problems we have today are Christians that have drink problems. And here you find a wonderful man of God, a type of Christ, falling into sin, and here you see it destroying one of his sons. His son jumped on the chance to destroy his father's integrity, his father's character, and in the end, he got cursed. But Noah died at 950 years, and yet he's still saved. He's in Heaven today.

CHAPTER 10

Okay. Just before I get into the tenth chapter – and I'm not going to read every verse in this part of Scripture. You can read it at your own leisure. But we finished the ninth chapter looking at the fall of Noah. And, of course, Noah's fall didn't just impact himself; it also impacted his middle child. He fell; he fell through his father's fall. And that is the problem with sin. Sin is contagious, and 1 Corinthians 10:12 Paul says, **"Wherefore let him that thinketh he standeth take heed lest he fall."** No matter how spiritual, no matter how strong you think you are or even if you are a strong believer in the faith, your flesh is always going to pull you down, and your fall – and you will fall. Mark my words, you will fall sooner or later, but the point I want to make is that when you do fall, just make sure that those around you don't follow you too. And this can also feed into the issue of liberty. A person's liberty can cause somebody else to stumble. And I've spoken about this on previous videos. But I just wanted to make that brief footnote before I get to the tenth chapter. And, like I say, I won't look at every verse in the tenth chapter, just pick out a few verses and offer some thoughts as I go through it.

VERSE 1: "Now these are the generations of the sons of Noah, Shem, Ham, and Japheth: and unto them were sons born after the flood."

VERSE 2 is interesting, the sons of Japheth, Gomer and Magog. It's interesting that the genealogy starts with the youngest of the three sons. Normally you start with the oldest, but in this part of Scripture, we're going to find that Japheth is the father of the Gentiles, and you're going to get two lines: You're going to get the Gentile line, and you're going to get the Messianic Jewish line. And there's a third line also, but verse

2 speaks about Magog, and he's found in Ezekiel. And many people consider Magog to be part of a Russian or a Chinese invasion into Israel at the end of the Millennium just before the eternal state is ushered in.

VERSE 5: "By these were the isles of the Gentiles divided in their lands; every one after his tongue, after their families, in their nations."

So if you're a non-Jew, then your great, great times 200 grandfather would be Japheth. And here you find an unbroken link, an unbroken chain going right back to the first father, if you will, of the Gentiles. And I just want to say one other thing that if you are a Roman Catholic and you believe in this unbroken papal line going back to Peter, then just think again, because not only have you had several popes that have come from, let's say, financially well-off backgrounds – aristocrats – and those people were able to buy the papacy and put their man on the throne, but you've had women, you've even had children on the throne. But the point I want to make is this that even the Jews, they had their high priest from Aaron right up to Caiaphas, and when the Lord Jesus Christ arrived on the earth, none of those high priests knew and believed on Him. Yes, you had Nicodemus; yes, you had Joseph of Arimathea, but the high priests' unbroken line going back to Aaron didn't see, didn't know who Jesus Christ was. In fact, Jesus wasn't even ordained among the "priesthood" of His day. He was ordained by an itinerant preacher in the desert. Of course, that's John the Baptist.

So, again, you've got to look at these things quite carefully. If you fall into organised religion, then you expect organised religion to ordain you; you expect organised religion to give you a sense of respect, a sense of authority, and yet in the New Testament, when the Son of God – very God, very man – when He arrived, He didn't go to Caiaphas for His ordination. He didn't go to Ananias; He didn't go to any of the high priests of His day, but He went to a man in the desert. And you can imagine how the snobs of John's day felt about that. But, anyway, Japheth is the father of the Gentiles, and, as I say, if you're living today, then he's your great, great how ever many generations grandfather.

VERSE 6: "And the sons of Ham; Cush, and Mizraim, and Phut, and Canaan."

Canaan, of course, goes back to Cain, the first murderer in the Bible, so already you see that Ham isn't in good company. In fact, not only is Ham cursed, but Nimrod is going to come from his line. And like I said in the other video, the Antichrist quite possibly will come from this line of Jews too.

VERSES 8-9: "And Cush begat Nimrod: he began to be a mighty one in the earth. He was a mighty hunter before the LORD: wherefore it is said, Even as Nimrod the mighty hunter before the LORD."

Some people think that Nimrod is a black man. I don't know where they get that from. Nothing in Scripture suggests that he is. But whoever he was, he was a very powerful man, and I would put it to you that he is a type of the Antichrist – not the first type. The first type was Cain. Cain killed his brother prematurely. And, of course, Abel is a type of Christ, a good man who died in his prime, and he was killed by his brother. There is Scripture in the New Testament where Paul says that the Jews killed the Lord Jesus Christ. Yes, the Romans physically put Him on the cross and they physically banged the nails into His hands and into His feet, but they did it under duress from the Jews. So already you're seeing an early type of Saviour, if you will, in Abel in a limited sense, of course, but Cain linking up to Nimrod as a type of Antichrist. And, of course, go back to Genesis 3, and the main Antichrist in the Bible, of course, is Satan, Lucifer, the devil.

VERSE 10: "And the beginning of his kingdom was Babel" – which means confusion.

Interesting that Nimrod is linked to a kingdom called Babel, and Cain, once again, back in Genesis 4 goes out from the presence of the Lord and dwells in the land of Nod, and in 17 it says **"he builded a city, and called the name of the city, after the name of his son, Enoch."** So here you can see two types of the Antichrist building physical kingdoms, much like the world system that we see today which is controlled by the devil. And that's why the Lord calls us out of the world. We are in the world but not of the world, and Jesus said that His Kingdom wasn't of this world. So already you're getting a picture of a physical world and a spiritual world. We will live in this physical world until we die, but spiritually, our conversation is in Heaven.

VERSE 11: Out of that land went forth Asshur, and builded Nineveh" –

Of course, Nineveh fits into Jonah's generation. Again, Jonah from Galilee like Jesus, although Jesus was born in Bethlehem but He was raised in Galilee, and Jonah goes to the Gentiles of his generation and preaches to them and they repent and get saved – many, many, types in the Scripture. And here Asshur builds Nineveh.

VERSE 19: "And the border of the Canaanites was from Sidon, as thou comest to Gerar, unto Gaza; as thou goest, unto Sodom, and Gomorrah" –

Now, of course, we know where Gaza is today. Gaza is occupied by several groups within groups which are called Palestinians, and their founder was a man called Yasser Arafat who was an Egyptian. And he was a thorn in the side of the Jews for many, many years. And, of course, he's dead now, but for all of his years being a terrorist, being a thorn in the side of the Jewish state, it's pretty interesting that none of the

Muslim neighbours did much for him. In fact, he was quite unpopular. But the one thing that they all did support, did like him for was being a thorn in the side of the Jews. And I've often thought that if Saudi Arabia was so keen to help their Muslim brethren, they would scoop them all up from the Palestinian "territories" and put them in Saudi Arabia. Saudi Arabia is a huge country. There's many, many square miles of unused land, and they could quite easily repatriate all of the Muslims from the Palestinian areas and put them in Saudi Arabia, but it won't happen.

But here Gaza is linked to Sodom and Gomorrah, and, of course, Sodom and Gomorrah is the infamous towns and cities which the Lord destroyed.

VERSE 20: "These are the sons of Ham, after their families, after their tongues, in their countries, and in their nations."

So if you go back to 19, 18, 17, 16, 15, 14, 13, 12, 11, go back to probably 8, you can see the genealogies quite clear. And just keep one other thing in mind: Just because these are all men listed doesn't mean that there weren't any daughters that were also born to these three men and their sons. There probably were. But this is dealing with the men. Of course, the Bible does focus on the men in the sense that man was born in the image of God as was woman also. But other parts of the Scriptures you get men and women in the genealogy. You get it in the Gospel of Matthew, of course, and Luke also has a few women in there too. But here Moses is going to focus on the men. So don't read into that as being sexist in any way. It's not. It's just dealing with the heads of the family. As Christ is the head of the body, the husband is head of the family.

VERSE 21: Unto Shem also, the father of all the children of Eber, the brother of Japheth the elder, even to him were children born."

Twenty-two, 23, 24, 25 going down to, let's say, 31, more names are mentioned there, and I shan't read them all. You can do that at your own leisure.

VERSES 31-32: "These are the sons of Shem, after their families, after their tongues, in their lands, after their nations. These are the families of the sons of Noah, after their generations, in their nations: and by these were the nations divided in the earth after the flood."

Pre Genesis 11, everybody spoke with one language, and Scripture says in the last days, they'll all speak with one language.

So you've got three lines here. You've got Ham, Japheth, and Shem, and it's imperative that you know which line you are of. And although we are all physical descendents of at least one of these three men, we are not spiritual descendents of God until we are born again. And Galatians 3 says, **"For ye are all the children of God by faith in Christ Jesus"** (v. 26.) So until you are born again, you are not a child of God; you are a child of the devil through your Adamic fall. And, yes, you are, as I say, a physical descendent of Ham, Japheth, or Shem, but that doesn't make you a child of God until you are born again. And I'll give you one more reference, John 1:11: **"He came unto his own, and his own received him not. But as many as received him, to them gave he power to become the sons of God, even to them that believe on his name "** (vv. 11-12.) So until you believe on His name, you are not a son of God, you're not a child of God, but you're under the judgment, you're under the condemnation. And, like I say, you are by your fall, by your Adamic nature a child of the devil.

So I plead with you today if you're not saved to get saved and become a child of the Lord and be a fruitful, faithful son or daughter of the God of the Bible.

CHAPTER 11

Okay. Well, this will be the final video that I do on the book of Genesis, at least for the time being. Maybe next year I will return and continue on from the twelfth chapter. But the first batch of videos, I wanted to focus, really, on the first eleven chapters of Genesis. And many thanks to those of you that have started with me and have finished with me.

Just a quick point I wanted to highlight before I get to the eleventh chapter. Chapter 4, a man called Lamech is mentioned, and he's a great, great grandson of Cain, and, of course, he's in that cursed line which the Antichrist, I believe, will come from. But Lamech, like his great, great grandfather, wasn't only a murderer but he was also the first polygamist in Scripture, and he's also the father of music. And if you go through Ezekiel, you'll find that Satan is also linked with music. Just a point I wanted to share with you. I think everything in Scripture is written for a purpose and for a reason, and it's down to all Christians to be faithful Bereans, studying the Scriptures, searching the Scriptures and using it as a shield and also for our own edification.

The eleventh chapter has got a couple of genealogies in it dealing with Shem, and I won't read them all. I haven't got time to. So like the tenth chapter, I'll just pick out the verses which I think are the most important and invite you, the listener, to read the entire chapter at your own leisure.

VERSE 1: "And the whole earth was of one language, and of one speech."

If you go to the book of Zephaniah, chapter 3 verse 9, and the Scripture says: **"For then will I turn to the people a pure language, that they** may all call upon the name of the LORD, to serve him with one consent." This is eschatological, no doubt about it, and this verse, tied in with the eleventh chapter, suggests to me that somehow in the Tribulation or late Tribulation the people of the earth are going to have one language. Now, I can't really expound any more on that, but these verses can be cross referenced together, perhaps a bigger or more clear picture. But when I read this earlier on, I thought Zephaniah 3:9 also from the tenth chapter needed to be cross referenced and put to you.

VERSE 2: "And it came to pass, as they journeyed from the east, that they found a plain in the land of Shinar; and they dwelt there."

New Testament, the wise men came from the East. It's quite unusual for those in the East to travel to the West or anywhere, really, because in antiquity, the East was where all the knowledge was. And you can imagine Herod being in Jerusalem and this massive army arrive and going around everywhere asking everybody where the King of the Jews was born. And I just want to say one quick point that of all the biblical films that I've ever watched, nearly all of them omit the fact that the wise men wouldn't have travelled on their own. They would have had a big army, possibly a few hundred men. They were carrying gold, frankincense, and myrrh, plus other valuables. So they are like modern-day ambassadors, if you will, and modern-day ambassadors living in dangerous countries travel in a large security detail. But here it says that they travelled from the East.

VERSES 3-4: "And they said one to another, Go to, let us make brick, and burn them throughly. And they had brick for stone, and slime had they for morter. And they said, Go to, let us build us a city and a tower, whose top may reach unto heaven; and let us make us a name, lest we be scattered abroad upon the face of the whole earth."

Nobody can be too dogmatic about the exact timing of the pyramids when they were built, and it's possible that these early builders were trying to either mimic the pyramids, or the Egyptians were trying to mirror what these guys are doing. But either way, it's going to be in vain. And Jesus said in John 10 that thieves and robbers came before Him, and He was the only way to be saved. So when you have people coming together trying to reach deity, how ever they would envisage it, if it's not done in light of Scripture, then it's vain, totally vain.

VERSE 5: "And the LORD came down to see the city and the tower, which the children of men builded."

Capital "L," capital "O," capital "R," capital "D" – that's Jehovah God. And verse 7 tells me that is the triune God, a reference to the Trinity.

VERSES 6-7: "And the LORD said, Behold, the people is one, and they have all one language; and this they begin to do: and now nothing will be restrained from them, which they have imagined to do. Go to, let us go down, and there confound their language, that they may not understand one another's speech."

Again, Father, Son, and the Holy Spirit built the earth from nothing. I've shown you that from the first chapter. They resurrected the Lord Jesus Christ together. But here the triune God is literally on the earth monitoring what's happening, and He's going to deal with this rebellion, this high treason, as the Lord sees it.

VERSE 8: "So the LORD scattered them abroad from thence upon the face of all the earth: and they left off to build the city."

One of the commandments was to go forth, multiply, and populate the earth. The book of Acts tells us that the Lord sent the apostles out to preach the Gospel, and one of the ways that He was able to get His apostles to spread out was persecution. The Roman Emperors didn't want the Jews in Rome, so they expelled them. That forced them out. Pressure from Israel also pushed them out. And here the Lord Himself has said, "I don't want you to stay here; I want you to go out;

there's a whole world out there." And they were all hanging around Mesopotamia, and the Lord said, "No, you're going to spread out." And eventually the twelve tribes of Israel are going to take the world.

VERSE 9: "Therefore is the name of it called Babel; because the LORD did there confound the language of all the earth: and from thence did the LORD scatter them abroad upon the face of all the earth."

The subject of speaking in tongues comes to mind when I look at the eleventh chapter. Acts 2 tells us that when the apostles spoke in tongues, their own brethren that were there noted the language that was being spoken – many different languages, of course, and they were spoken in their own tongues. Paul says in 1 Corinthians that if somebody speaks in tongues, there must be an interpreter. The interpreter is there to explain to the congregation what is being said. And if somebody goes into your meeting and everyone is speaking in tongues and there's no interpreter, then it's like a mad house.

Tongues were for a sign to the Jews and they were given to the saved Jews as a rebuke to the unsaved Jews, whereas prophecy edifies the entire church. Today's tongues are predominantly gibberish and mean nothing whatsoever. There's also a danger that you fall into the demonic realm when you start blabbering in tongues. But if you are into tongues, if you think tongues are still applicable, then Acts 2 tells you that they are a known language, and 1 Corinthians makes it very clear that only two or three men would speak in tongues at any one time or it's with an interpreter present – never women. Women don't speak in tongues nor do they interpret. They can pray; they can prophesy according to the eleventh chapter, but they don't speak in tongues. Tongues was given to men in the New Testament to proclaim the Gospel, and, like I say, it was a sign to the Jewish people. But today's modern tongues movement doesn't even modestly resemble what we find in the Scripture.

Ten, 11, 12, 13 going right down to 25 deals with the line of Shem, and, again, Shem is a Messianic man. In fact, I've got a chart here which I'm just going to quickly read to you. Shem, Abraham, Lot, Rebekah, Isaac, and even Esau, of course, come from that line of Shem. Jesus Christ also comes in that line. Esau is a bit of a difficult one because he gets involved with Edom, marries a Hittite, an Ishmaelite, and, of course, Baal and Mohammed come from that line. So he starts out well, Esau; he's in the right line, shall we say. But Scripture says, **"Jacob have I loved, but Esau have I hated"** (Rom. 9:13.) And the Muslims claim that Mohammad is linked to Ishmael, which is clearly found in the Scripture, and he's also directly linked to Esau.

So Shem, Abraham, Rebekah, Isaac, and Esau come from Shem, but the curse line – one more time, this cursed line, Ham, Nimrod, Babel, Nineveh, Philistine, Sodom and Gomorrah, and Dan – again, Dan, a lot of people think, is the tribe which will produce the Antichrist in the last days.

VERSE 26: "And Terah lived seventy years, and begat Abram, Nahor, and Haran."

They would be the brothers of Abraham, of course.

VERSE 27: "Now these are the generations of Terah: Terah begat Abram, Nahor, and Haran; and Haran begat Lot."

But Abraham was Lot's uncle. And some Catholics will use this to prove that the brethren of the Lord spoken of in the Gospels are not His physical brethren but His cousins, but that won't work because Genesis clearly tells you that his brother produced Lot. And just because they're called brothers doesn't mean they were biological brothers - It's simply an expression. We have brothers in the Lord. We call this person Brother Such and Such. He's not my literal brother; he's my spiritual brother. So just read the Scriptures a bit more carefully, and you won't make the same blunder.

VERSE 28: "And Haran died before his father Terah in the land of his nativity, in Ur of the Chaldees."

Job also comes from the city of Ur, and he too would be a type of Christ. He's also a type of a suffering Jew in the Tribulation, and he gets delivered, of course, at the end of Job. But all these lines are linked up quite nicely, but you've got to study the Scriptures to get them in the right order.

Twenty-nine talks about Abram and his brother taking wives, and, of course, Sarai becomes Sarah later on, which means princess. Thirty says she was barren and had no child.

VERSES 31-32: "And Terah took Abram his son, and Lot the son of Haran his son's son, and Sarai his daughter in law, his son Abram's wife; and they went forth with them from Ur of the Chaldees, to go into the land of Canaan; and they came unto Haran, and dwelt there. And the days of Terah were two hundred and five years: and Terah died in Haran."

And that concludes the eleventh chapter. And, like I say, I might return to this book in the New Year. But my final point would be that as Christians, as Biblicists, we need to defend the creation account; we need to defend the integrity of the inspiration and the preservation of the Scripture. We need to stand firm on faith through Christ alone, Jesus' deity, the triunity of God and His exclusivity. He is the only way that man is ever going to be saved, and I believe every Bible-believing Christian in whatever way he or she has been gifted by the Lord has a duty and is minded to defend the creation account, the Scriptures, Jesus' deity, and His exclusivity. You need to repent and come to the

Son of God. And I think anything that falls short of those particular areas is a travesty. We are ambassadors for Christ, and the battle lines, I suggest, have been drawn. And I ask you: Where do you stand on these issues?

Also by James Battell

The Shocking History of the Jesuits (The Society of Jesus)
King James I of England: The King The Vatican Could Not Kill
The Hidden Truth About Freemasonry, The Catholic Church, And The Illuminati
Bible Prophecy Made Simple For Serious Students of Scripture
Did The Catholic Church Order Abraham Lincoln's Assassination?
Is Calvinism and the Doctrines of Grace Biblical?
The Book of Genesis Commentary (Chapters 1-11)
The Book of Genesis Commentary (Chapters 1-11)
Watchman Nee, Witness Lee, and Living Stream Ministry: A Critical Analysis of Their Identity as Cult or Church
What Is Speaking In Tongues And Is It Still For Today?
Ephesians Bible Commentary
The Book of Romans Commentary
Philemon Bible Study (Slavery In Scripture)